Restructuring the Foundations of Schools

The Role of ICTs in Elementary and Secondary Education

Restructuring the Foundations of Schools

The Role of ICTs in Elementary and Secondary Education

R C Krishnamurthy

AUTHORSPRESS

Worldwide Circulation through Authorspress Global Network
First Published 2005
by Authorspress

E-35/103, Jawahar Park
Laxmi Nagar, Delhi-110 092

e-mail: authorspress@yahoo.com

Typeset in NewCenturySchlbk by Chitra Computers

Restructuring the Foundations of Schools:
The Role of ICTs in Elementary and Secondary Education
ISBN 81-7273-276-7

Printed in India at Tarun Offset, Delhi.

Preface

ICT is an integrated tool in the students' and teachers' daily work, and also a channel for communication and guidance. In this book we are exploring how modern communication technology can support and increase the student acitivity, lead them to instructing their own knowledge and facilitate a more flexible system of practical training that gives the students tangible experiences with the profession they are in.

This book concerns how ICT can create new, open learning environments and their instrumental role in shifting the emphasis from a teacher-centred to a learner-centred environment; where teachers move from being the key source of information and transmitter of knowledge to becoming a collaborator and co-learner; and where the role of students changes from one of passively receiving information to being actively involved in their own learning. It also indicates that efforts to ensure equal access to educational opportunities and quality education for all must be accompanied by wide-ranging education reforms. Such reforms are not likely to succeed without addressing the new roles played by teachers in preparing students for an emerging knowledge-based and technology-driven society.

A school may have broader policies in place that will influence a technology plan, such as business policies that could include requirements for impact analyses, financial contingencies, or security safeguards. Classroom spaces were designed to reflect the traditional instructional style with little, if any, thought given to investigation-based, group learning, let alone fibre-optic cabling. This book gives a valuable information to create more flexible space for ICT use in classroom.

ICT have important roles to play in making school administration less burdensome and more effectively integrated to the official information flow about students, curricula, teachers, budgets and activities through the educational system information pipelines. School administrators are more accepting of ICT in a school, when they use it themselves. Therefore, provision should be made for this. Moreover, information space of school management should be integrated with learning and teaching space.

Many resources and training opportunities are available to help employees meet the technology standards, including school-based technology specialists. This book gives more opportunities to develop and apply new approaches and strategies for teaching and learning that integrate computers, internet-enabled collaborative learning, and related educational technologies with routine teaching and learning.

Contents

1

ICTs: New Tools for Education

During the nineteenth and twentieth centuries, new tools for storing and transmitting information appeared. Today, computer-centred ICT are extending and amplifying our capacity for computational operations, logical reasoning, heuristic search, and grasping of coherence and hidden interconnectedness in chaotic signals and disparate data. That is, a computer is never autonomous but rather connected to a growing number of electronic digital devices, aggregations and networks for data and information acquisition, storage, processing, distribution and multimedia delivery. All these entities are subsumed under the generic name of ICT.

Signals and images in the physical world are either continuous or analogue. To be stored, transmitted, and processed by modern ICT, they must be transformed into digital, or discrete, signals. The simplest example of discretisation is measurement. When you measure length, weight, or time, you transform an analogue value into a digital one: the result is a finite sequence of digits.

1.1. Components of ICT

The components of ICT are the computer itself, storage media, and input and output devices.

1.1.1. Computers

The computer is a universal information processor. In theory, any kind of information processing can be done on any computer but, in reality, this is not true. A specific task for a specific computer may require too much time, or the computer's memory may be too small. Computers process information in the form of electric signals. In other existing technologies, simple information processing can be done also in the form of air or liquid streams. There are attempts to produce computers that use light processing, or biochemical mechanisms similar to that of living organisms, but these approaches are at a premature stage.

1.1.1.1. CPU

Information processing is done by computer hardware. The most important components of computers are (electronic) semiconductors, similar to the components of radio or TV, but much more sophisticated. The number of electronic elements inside these components can be counted in millions. These elements are joined together to form integrated circuits (IC), commonly referred to as microchips, or simply chips. The core device in any computer, called the central processing unit or CPU, does all information processing.

Today the CPU occupies a metal box in which you can see dozens of integrated circuits, wires, and cables connecting them. The main IC in the CPU is the processor itself, which does most of the active task of processing, including adding numbers, comparing strings of symbols, sending information to memory, retrieving it from memory and, very importantly, reacting to signals from the outside. The work a computer depends not only on its constitution as an electronic device, but also on the information stored in it or that it receives while in operation. This information can be considered as instructions that tell the computer what to do, and is called software.

Information is stored, transmitted, and processed in the form of strings of zeros and ones. The input of information into a computer usually involves the transformation of images or sounds into digital and discrete strings. The output involves the reverse transformation. These components of hardware and software responsible for these transformations and making them perceptible to the human senses, are called interfaces. Computer information is stored in special types of IC, called storage or memory chips. A computer's speed is an important factor in its performance. It is measured in MHz, which refers to the number of changes inside a computer that can take place in one second.

1.1.1.2. Monitor

An important component of any modern computer used by a human being (and for this reason called a personal computer), is the screen or monitor. Monitors not only display information but can also support direct interaction. For example, if you need to make a technical drawing of a particular detail with a computer, you move your hand equipped with one of many input devices, to create a line or activate a detail on the screen. The whole system of using physical movements to manipulate information and present this manipulation in intuitive screen images is called graphical user interface or GUI.

The CPU is connected with other ICT devices via communication channels. The most common communication channel is a cable plugged into a computer at one end, and to another device at the other end. The cables and sockets can cause problems, including incompatibility of sockets in the case of connecting your computer to a local telephone line abroad. A popular alternative to cables is wireless (radio-frequency or infra-red) connection. To simplify the graphic presentations, we do not include cables in the pictures, and say more about these connectors in the sections that follow.

Computers that are placed on the desk of a clerk, student, or teacher are called desktop computers. Sometimes, however, the computer itself is placed under the desk with the monitor and keyboard on top. These computers usually weigh several kilograms, with the monitor usually being the much heavier component. Other computers are portable or mobile. Their weight and size permit them to be carried comfortably. Computers of a size and weight of a large notebook, which is easy to carry, are called notebooks (formerly, laptops).

Today's notebooks weigh as little as 1-4 kg. Computers the size of one's palm, and weighing less than 1 kg, are called palm computers, handhelds, or palms. All such computers are called personal computers, or PCs, because they are intended for individual usage. CPUs today are very small. We can say that for most school applications the size of a typical CPU is not a limitation. On the other hand, in some classroom situations, the size of the whole computer matters. If we place a monitor on a student's desk, it must be large enough to be comfortably visible, yet small enough to leave space for student work.

Electricity is needed to run a computer and its related devices. The power consumption for a desktop computer is typically 100-500 watts. In many countries, this resource is widely available, but in others it is still a problem. For them, alternative power sources such as solar batteries, wind generators, and accumulators (rechargeable batteries), as well as UPS (Uninterruptible Power Supply), should be considered in the planning of ICT implementation. Solar batteries, for example, cost a few dollars and can supply a palm computer with energy, provided they are exposed to sunlight a couple of hours a day.

Portable computers can use the same power line as desktop computers. However, it is much more convenient to have a portable computer that can function, for a while at least, with rechargeable batteries. These can support the computer for a few hours, and then need to be recharged from a power source. In the best cases, recharging takes much less time than the computer needed to use up its power, and recharging can occur while the computer is in use. A bad aspect about accumulators, apart from their weight and considerable cost, is that, if used intensively, they last only a few months. Even in the best cases, a rechargeable batteries' life is much shorter than the life of the computer itself.

In many cases, the modern processors that have appeared over the last few years require more energy to run than the older ones. Roughly speaking, every action of the CPU needs a minimal amount of energy to be used. If the processor works faster, the same amount of energy is used in a shorter time. As the computer runs, this energy dissipates in the outside environment in the form of heat, and so computers come equipped with special cooling mechanisms like fans.

1.1.2. Peripherals

For the best utilisation of ICT in education, a teacher needs a wide range of devices connectable to a computer, and these are referred to as peripherals. The major categories of peripherals are devices for:

i) *Input*: alphanumeric keyboard, musical keyboard, microphone, taperecorder, tablet and stylus, scanner, digital photo camera, video camera, sensors, and probes.

ii) *Output*: monitor, printer, projector, headphones, speakers.

iii) *Control*: motors, lights for robotics construction kit, and sensors.

iv) *Communication*: modems, communication lines, satellite and local network equipment, and wireless networks.

Having a wide range of peripherals for educational and general use is more important in a school than the number of computers. Different components of a computer as well as peripheral devices need to be connected via channels for information flow. In most computers today, cables do this, but wireless connection is increasingly possible as well, which then requires, of course, that the device has its own source of energy (usually, power line or batteries).

1.1.3. Storage

Information is stored in integrated memory circuits or memory chips in the computer's CPU. However, there are other ways to store information. These other means differ in capacity (the amount of information they can store) and access speed (how fast the information can be retrieved).

Stored information can be retrieved and, in some cases, changed. Read-only memory (ROM) means that the user cannot change any retrieved information. The cost of storing information is constantly and rapidly decreasing. The key storage devices currently are flash cards, magnetic tapes and discs, and optical discs.

1.1.3.1. Flash cards

Additional memory chips—so-called flash cards—can be easily inserted into and removed from the body of current computers. They do not require batteries to keep information stored. The capacity of one card today is in the range of 10MB to 1GB and access is fast enough for most applications. Flash cards are widely used in digital cameras and other applications. They are rapidly replacing discs. Some versions of ROM cards are used in game consoles.

1.1.3.2. Magnetic tapes

Magnetic tapes, similar to those used in tape-recorders, can be used for storing digital information as well. To read or write information on a tape, a special device similar to a tape-recorder is used, called a tape drive. The drive can be external to a computer or placed inside the CPU box. The capacity of a tape can be up to 10 GB and even more. Access speed, however, is slow, which can be critical for certain applications, though this is less important for most school uses. Magnetic tapes are rewritable.

1.1.3.3. Magnetic discs

The idea of disc storage can be traced back to gramophone recordings at the beginning of the twentieth century. Information on those discs was permanently stored in the form of small mechanical (geometrical) changes in the surface of the disc. Some of today's versions of disc storage use a magnetic principle similar to tapes, and these discs are rewritable. Discs with the capacity of about 1MB are also called diskettes; you can insert them into a drive (disk-drive), or remove them. It may take up to a minute for a computer to read from or write to a diskette.

Newer discs have a capacity of up to 1GB. The competition from flash cards (see above) is strong. Discs with even greater capacity are mounted on their own drive, and these are usually called hard discs. Their capacity is in the order of 10GB to 1000GB. The access time for hard discs is fast enough for most applications.

1.1.3.4. Optical discs

Information can also be stored on a disc as an optical trace. This principle is exploited in compact discs (CD), widely used now for storing music. The capacity of a CD-ROM is approximately 1GB. Access speed may not be fast enough for some applications involving sound or moving pictures. Rewritable CDs and rewritable DVDs have appeared in recent years.

1.1.4. Input Devices

The most common way to input information into computers is by human hand through a variety of devices: keyboards, the mouse, graphical tablets, and touch screens.

1.1.4.1. Keyboards

The most important input device for computers currently is the keyboard, which serves mostly for text input, and, to a large extent, imitates the keyboards of typewriters. The computer has many advantages over a typewriter, even apart from its more sophisticated software and other applications. The first of these is how easy it makes it to change, delete or insert any word or phrase. The next is the ability to copy any text fragment and to move it as a solid object anywhere within a text, or to another text, usually referred to as cut-and-paste. Touch-typing (not looking to the keyboard and using 10 fingers) is a useful skill in the educational context today. Students can learn touch-typing faster than handwriting; they can type faster than they can write; and the results are more attractive and much easier to edit and revise.

Extensive work with the keyboard, however, sometimes causes muscular tension and requires special precautions, which students and teachers rarely take (see the chapter 4 on health problems associated with computers). Newer ergonomic keyboards are becoming more prevalent, as is the use of alternative methods of writing such as script and speech recognition. Different arrangements of characters on the keyboard could make typing more effective.

A radically new tool, called the Twiddler, is an ergonomic handheld, touch-type keypad designed for chord keying, which means that like a piano you press one or more keys at a time. Each key combination generates a unique character or command. Due to resistance to change, widespread adoption of these tools does not look probable. Keyboards of notebooks are usually built into the book. Keyboards are not usually built into palm computers. Sometimes a keyboard is represented by a screen image on which you type by touching keys with the tip of a special pen. Sometimes, lightweight unfolding keyboards are used for palm text input.

1.1.4.2. Mouse

To manipulate screen objects, you need to point, choose, grab, and open them. In today's computers, these operations are usually done with a special instrument, which indicates an object on the screen and moves it as a solid body. This instrument is called a mouse, a handheld, traditionally grey, plastic body that you move on the table-top, which is usually covered by a small mat called a mousepad, designed to improve the movement of the mouse. As you move the mouse, a small object (an arrow, for example), called a cursor, moves on the screen, mimicking the mouse's movements on the table.

The mouse has buttons that help you to extract, pick up, and manipulate objects. You move the cursor to an object and click a button; the object now is attached to the cursor and can be moved. If you click another button, the object opens up. These actions are part of GUI or the graphical user interface. There are other devices to transform movements on screen into information manipulation inside the computer similar to the mouse. They all act similarly, but the physical movements of a human hand working with them can be quite different.

A handheld mouse, not lying on the table, can have a small gyroscope inside, and is useful when you show something to others on a big screen. A trackpad is a small panel (about 3 by 4 cm) over which you move your index finger to control the cursor. A trackball is a ball about the size of an egg embedded into a panel, which you can rotate. A joystick is a small lever (as in a car transmission gearshift) used mostly in computer games. There are also very small joysticks inside some keyboards called trackpoints, which you can push and deflect with your finger. These are also used as the mouse part of the Twiddler mentioned above, where the trackpoint is controlled with the thumb. Wireless mice that have no moving parts are more reliable and have become more popular. Among them there are handheld mice that you do not place on a table but move in 3D space.

1.1.4.3. Graphical tablets

Another type of input is to draw or write with a pen. The difference between a computer pen or stylus and an ordinary one is that the computer pen moves over a special surface called a graphical tablet, and the trace of the move can be represented on screen. The computer can also measure levels of pressure. With appropriate software, a computer can imitate almost all existing drawing techniques and create some exciting new ones. The computer is very useful for technical drawing—now, mostly part of computer-aided design or CAD.

1.1.4.4. Touch screens

Another promising type of device combines seeing with touching, allowing you, for example, to outline an object on the screen with your finger and then move it to a different position with the same finger. This is already achieved with touch screens. A finger cannot indicate a very small object on a screen. However, this limitation can be relaxed by using a stylus on the screen (a kind of pen or pencil designed for this kind of interaction). Touch screens can work well and are more intuitive for small children, but are not widely used. One reason for this is their cost, which is higher than an ordinary screen and mouse. Nevertheless, they are the most popular devices in most information kiosks and in palm computers.

1.1.5. Visual Information

In the mid-nineteenth century, photography was invented as a means of fixing and storing visual information in an external medium using a chemical process. In the 1930s, devices were introduced that transform visual information into electronic form for immediate transmission via electromagnetic waves: TV technology. In the 1950s, simultaneously with computer technology, methods to record and play back analogue TV and still images appeared: the videotape. At the end of the twentieth century, digital photography and digital TV became an integral part of computer-based ICT.

1.1.5.1. Cameras

Cameras store or transmit visual images. The photographic camera stores a still image on photographic film for further chemical development. Instead of putting an image onto a film, a digital camera places it in the computer's memory, or in the memory of the camera for transmission to a computer for storage or direct printing afterwards. An interesting application of digital cameras is the projection of a small image (such as a bug, for instance) onto a large screen. Nowadays, digital cameras can store video images also.

1.5.1.2. Scanners

Scanners look very like copying machines, but are smaller and usually work more slowly. Instead of producing a paper copy of an image, a scanner transmits an image in digital form to a connected computer. Scanners can be used to transform information from a paper source—a text, an image from a book, a drawing, or a photograph into a digital image. Additional devices can be used for scanning 35mm slides. There are also handheld pensize scanners that you can move over a line of text or a bar code for input or storage inside the scanner. Special 3D (three dimensional) scanners can produce scanned images viewable from different angles.

1.1.5.3. Optical character recognition

A special situation occurs when an image is a text (or text combined with graphics) in printed or handwritten form. In this case, the image of the text can be transformed (converted) into a computer text file that can be processed as one does other texts in the computer (e.g. insert a phrase; change a shorter name to a longer one, and so on). This process of transformation from picture to text uses sophisticated software called Optical Character Recognition (OCR).

1.1.6. Aural Input

As with visual information, non-electronic, that is mechanical technologies, were developed first to store sounds. Then, electronic technologies were developed to transmit sounds (telephone, radio), followed by electronic media and tools to store sounds (tape-recorders).

1.1.6.1. Microphones

Microphones transform sounds into electric signals for storage or transmission. There are different types of microphones and different ways to work with them:

i) A microphone can be fixed in a stand in front of a speaker who is standing or sitting.

ii) Speakers can hold a microphone in their hand.

iii) A lightweight microphone can be attached to a speaker's clothes.

Information converted by a microphone into electrical signals can be transmitted via a wired or wireless channel to other devices.

1.1.6.2. Sound recording

Sound can be recorded with a usual tape-recorder. To process sounds with a computer, you need to convert them into digital form. A microphone can also be plugged into a computer directly. In this case, the computer serves as a recorder. Digital recorders to store sound in digital form using flash cards are becoming increasingly popular. Modern computers can easily store hours of speech. Music recordings, processed and compressed by computer (in MP3 format, for example), occupy very little memory. The spread of this process, on CDs and through the internet, is changing the recording industry and affecting mass culture.

During the last few years, software has been developed that allows a computer to transform human speech into a text file similar to the conversion of handwriting as discussed above. This transformation can be done with a level of quality that makes it adequate for educational applications, and is useful, for instance, in learning English.

1.1.6.3. Sensor

A sensor generates an electrical signal that is then usually transmitted to a computer via an interface. More sophisticated sensors can measure such parameters, store, and display them, even if a sensor is not connected to a computer. This can be done by individual sensors or by what is called a data logger, a special device or small box to collect and store data. The content of measurements can then be transferred to a computer. Very promising in school education is the growing number of sen—sors—from those that measure acid rain and heavy metal oxides ratio in potable water to the Global Positioning System (GPS), which allows anyone to find geographic coordinates and related information on the earth's surface.

1.1.7. Output

Output refers to information that a computer sends to a human user, or, sometimes, to other technical devices.

1.1.7.1 Monitor screen

The most immediate computer output is a visual image on the monitor screen. In most computer applications, the image on the screen is discrete, and consists of millions of picture elements called pixels. The colour and brightness of each element appears as a combination of three colours called RGB for red (R), green (G), and blue (B), with varying brightness for each colour. In reality, for every particular screen, each of these three basic colours consists of the entire spectrum of light waves. The brightness (intensity) of the three basic colours is coded by a symbol from a finite range. The symbol and the range of old computers were just one byte (8 bits).

Today, colours are usually presented by 3-byte coding (24-bits) representing millions of colours) or 4-byte coding (32-bits) rep-resenting billions of colours. The latest technology appears to be able to capture all possible variations in colour. In normal light conditions, the human eye can recognise differences in brightness (contrast) in the range of 1:10,000 or even more. Existing output screens can provide differences in brightness up to 1:1,000. In many cases—in most school conditions, for example—ambient light reduces the contrast radically, and so teachers need to adjust conditions of vision and the absolute brightness of screens.

TV screens similar to, or the same as, computer screens used today, offer a slightly different way of presenting information—partly digital, partly analogue. Generally, today's TVs produce less detailed images than good computers, though the newest TV standards have images of the same quality as good computer images. This improved definition is called HDTV (high definition TV). The move to HDTV is accompanied by a trend to change the aspect ratio (the fraction of screen width to its height) from 3:4 to 9:16, which is the ratio usually seen on cinema screens.

Theoretically, the limits of a visual image are the limits of human perception, which means that the screen can provide all the colour and brightness variations in the smallest details in the visible field (and even pay attention to twoeye stereoscopic vision). In reality, existing screen images are somewhat more limited: they have less detail than the human eye can grasp. The human retina has about 300 million cells whereas the best screens today have about 10 million pixels. Eventually, there is a natural limit to the improvement in quality that the human eye can perceive, which will occur when the computer screen is large enough to cover the prime area of clear vision and, at the same time, the smaller pixel-like details are no longer seen separately.

In some countries and regions, there has been concern over monitor safety. This problem has two aspects. The first is image quality. Older monitors (especially, bad quality TV sets that are sometimes used as monitors) have a blinking, non-stable image, and can cause considerable eye tension. The second issue is the radiation (mainly, radio frequency) that the monitor emits. Presently, monitors are as safe as possible, especially in combination with other proper conditions such as attention to ambient light. One of the key parameters of image quality is refreshment rate, which by most standards, should not be less than 85 Hz. In many newer computer models, it is about 100 Hz.

The classical display technology is the cathode ray tube (CRT), used in most TVs as well as in most monitors. This device is limited by its large depth-dimension and weight. A safer and more comfortable alternative is the LCD (liquid crystal display) monitor, which takes up much less space on a desk, and is important for many classroom applications. They are more expensive than CRT monitors today, but the prices for a whole computer system are not dramatically different.

1.1.7.2. Projectors

Computer images can be projected onto a screen. Projection flourished in the cinema era. Pre-electronic projectors used transparent film with an image to be projected. The 35mm film can be used in a roll as in diaprojectors (almost non-existent today), or cut into slides for use in slide projectors. Today, all slides (or screens—information objects to be projected) can be made on computer or be input to a computer and presented on computer screen. Special software used for projection of screen images, constructing, and organising them is called presentation software. One of the popular software products here is Microsoft's PowerPoint.

Electronic technology has made it possible to project computer-generated images as well as images from a camera and from a VCR (video cassette recorder). The projected images, different from a computer monitor or TV screen, can be of any size. The only limitation here is that the brightness of the image is reduced proportionally to the area (or squared linear size) of the image. If the ambient light in a room is stronger than the projector's light, differences in colour and brightness of different parts of the image on the screen are not seen clearly enough or, in some cases, at all.

The projection device is usually called a multimedia projector or LCD-projector (indicating, not in all cases correctly, the technology used), or beamer. Projector technology has developed affordable solutions that are available now in many schools. A computer presentation or video image can be brought to any classroom using a portable screen (weighing less than 2 kg), a portable projector (less than 2 kg), and a computer (less than 2 kg). In fact, each of the items can weigh less than a kilogram. One of the important trends for monitors and projectors is standardisation of the digital interface between computer and the device. The DVI (Digital Video Interface) standard describes the digital interaction between monitor and computer.

1.1.7.3. Stereovision

The ability to see with two eyes is important for human perception in some cases. For example, stereovision is useful to estimate distance along with other instruments like accommodation, head movements, and relative size of objects. Accordingly, it is possible to improve perception on a computer by creating a stereoscopic output. This can be done with separate screens for each eye, or by showing on the screen alternating pictures for each of the eyes. Closing screens for eyes alternately can solve the problem of showing to each eye what is needed. The closing can be implemented, for example, by glasses in which the lenses are made out of liquid crystal and become transparent and opaque alternately.

1.1.7.4. Printers and plotters

A printer transforms screen images into images on paper, so-called hard copy. A natural consequence of this is a need for paper and ink. The problem of cost here can be serious for schools in particular, because it is so easy to generate printouts in large quantities.

Laser printers produce black and white images and text of good quality for all school applications at an affordable price. In fact, laser printers changed the appearance of the world of written text. Once, the quality of print correlated with the respectability of the author but this is no longer so since, at first glance, all printed papers look the same. Alternatives to laser printing are LED (lightemitting diodes) and ink-jet printing. These printers are used in schools as well, but do not provide any considerable advantage. The generation of printers before laser printers were so-called dot-matrix printers, which used principles similar in some respects to old typewriters with printer ribbon and mechanical impact.

Dot-matrix printers are useful if a school has poor quality paper or if you need to use wider paper or long rolls of paper (for banners, for instance). It is desirable also to have colour printers in schools. A little while ago, the price of colour printers and supplies was too high for most schools but, in recent times, the situation has changed and colour printing has become much more affordable.

A recent invention in printers is so-called Random Movement Printing Technology (RMPT). Printers using this technology can be the size of a computer mouse and used in the same way: randomly moving it over a sheet of paper of any size leaves text printed on it. A device similar to a printer in its functionality, but based on a different technology, is a plotter in which an image on paper appears, not as a combination of dots, but as a continuous line of ink.

1.1.7.5. Audio output

The audio channel is under-exploited in modern ICT in comparison with the visual channel. An important aspect of aural perception is locating the sound source using bi-aural (stereo-phonic) mechanisms. Two loudspeakers of mediocre quality are the most widespread audio output for consumer computers. Headphones can be used for stereo output as well. Some are better than others in quality of sound and the level of blocking of outside noise. Headphones can provide better quality than loudspeakers of the same price. In general, headphones are more useful for schools than speakers. Headphones can be coupled with a microphone.

1.1.7.6. Control applications

Control applications were among the most important applications of ICT before the advent of personal computers. Among specific cases are control of industrial machinery, power plants, and missiles. By contrast, personal computers mostly control output devices like printers. However, even this situation is changing, since a personal computer can, for example, be the control centre of an intelligent house, where the owner instructs the computer to operate all home appliances.

1.1.8. Communication Channels

Computers are connected to other ICT devices by communication channels that can be wired or wireless. In general, wired (cable) connection remains the more common type of connection. A cable connecting a computer to a peripheral can be used for three purposes:

i) to transfer energy (electrical current) to a peripheral;

ii) to transfer control signals to and from a peripheral (for example, a printer can receive a command "start printing", and send a feedback "notready", or "start sending the image to print", or "out of paper"); and

iii) to transfer input or output information (text to be printed to a printer, or sound to be digitised from a microphone).

It is common to transfer different electrical signals through one cable in several separate wires. (Actually, the same wire can be used for many signals simultaneously as well.) For different channels of communication, different cables are used. When we connect a cable to a computer or peripheral, we use sockets, sometimes called ports or plugs in the computer's box. A crucial issue in the use of cables is standardisation. Travellers, for instance, know well that about a dozen power plug standards exist internationally and perhaps a hundred telephone plug standards.

Fortunately, standardisation in the computer world is becoming more prevalent. At the same time, manufacturers are producing more and more new sockets. Consequently, when connecting a computer to external (peripheral) devices, one must be aware of such labels as PCMCIA, USB, IEEE 1394, and DVI. An important characteristic of a channel is the speed of transmission it allows. For some applications, including school ones, it is also important to plug in or unplug a peripheral device while the computer is working. Old interfaces often required the computer to be turned off while you plugged in or unplugged a device. The newer USB interface does not require turning off the computer while connecting a new device.

Using these channels can be critically important for schools, because they provide much needed flexibility. A channel allows computers to be moved between classrooms while keeping the network still operating. In the classroom, it allows children to sit where they are most comfortable without having to struggle with cables. Wireless connections can still be used between keyboard and computer. Brand names like Bluetooth, Airport, as well as standards of Wi-Fi (wireless fidelity), or IEEE 802.11, are used to describe common wireless interfaces. Wireless communication, however, has its limitations since, for example, infrared connection works well in a direct-sight situation only.

1.1.9. Networking

Computers linked to communicate and exchange information constitute a network. The most common standard of communication via wired local area network (LAN) is IEEE 802.3 (Ethernet is another name). It can be wired or wireless.

Sometimes a single computer called a server is dedicated to information storage and exchange for a network. Other computers are clients. Often, computational and storage power are concentrated in the server, and client computers are made as simple as possible. Such clients are called thin clients. These computers have few precise mechanical works (spinning discs) and a small and cheap display that is hard to break and easy to replace.

In the school context, relatively primitive computers can be useful when all that is needed is basic text processing. It may then be sufficient to have just a keyboard with simple electronics, small memory, four or eight lines of LCD and interfaces. The thin computer, also called a thick keyboard or smart keyboard, consists of a keyboard extended by a minimal display device to see what you are typing, and has a limited memory, an interface to transfer your text to a server or a printer, a processor to manage all of these, and a power supply (usually an inexpensive accumulator battery).

1.1.9.1. Internet

The next natural step is to link or network separate computers. Two computers can be linked via modem but this process is expensive if the computers are really distant from each other. We may compare this computer linking with the courier mail of the past, where a messenger brings a letter from one point to another. The high cost of this form of communication was reduced by the modern postal service. Developers of the internet (known also as the Net or the Web) thought similarly that having electronic post offices functioning automatically in many places would cut the costs of individual communications radically.

As with ordinary mail, one can move bulk mail between two major post offices in two cities as well as deliver individual letters locally. In the computer world, this is called email, and it was the starting point of the internet. Several important features contribute to making the internet the most democratic information medium today. Besides sending and receiving electronic mail, the internet provides an opportunity to place an information object (however complex and possibly linked to other objects) on a computer, give it an address, and make it available to a range of users who are also connected to the internet.

Hundreds of millions of people in every country of the world now use the internet. A popular way to communicate over the internet is to post information (usually text or pictures) to a personal or business homepage, or website. Another internet feature is user-groups who have access to bulletin boards—a collection of information on a specific topic that can be read and extended by members of a specific group with access. Emails move so quickly—in seconds from any sender to any receiver—that they allow for an exchange of information online (staying internet-connected, sending and receiving messages). This mode of communication is also called chat.

Today the internet is the biggest ever network channel and source of human information. Over the last decade, the internet has grown exponentially in numbers of participants and in the amount of information available. Access to the internet is possible, not only with the average personal computer, but also with simpler equipment called a network computer (a kind of thin client), which has an internet resource and connection but without computer software and storage. A TV set with a simple device like a Nintendo-SEGA game machine can be adapted to provide access to the internet. So can an enhanced telephone set.

1.1.9.2. Videoconferencing

The idea of combining telephones and TV communications has been tried for many years. The principal problems have not been so much technical as organisational, to do with infrastructure (allocating channels), and economic (it has been extremely expensive). In the last decade, however, computer algorithms and standards of compression, as well as channels of communication, have improved greatly. A roving video camera attached to a computer can automatically focus on a person speaking. Participants have microphones mounted on their desks and when they ask a question, the camera moves in to film them, and the image is displayed on a monitor screen. A human face and figure, slides, video, internet, whiteboard writing and drawing can all be seen on-site or transmitted via the internet. The result is an instant multimedia presentation.

For most educational institutions today, telephone lines and modems are the usual communications media for connecting with the internet. The speed of information transfer via telephone lines is usually below 56 Kbps (if the frequencies used are the same as for voice transmission). It is possible to transfer data and pictures and even low quality, live video signals via such channels. Telephone lines can also be used to transfer radio frequency signals to make transmission much faster, which is the technology used in digital subscriber lines (DSL).

An alternative is a radio channel via air (amateur short wave or another radiofrequency band, for example 2.4 GHz). An example is GPRS (General Packet Radio Service), a standard for wireless communications that runs at speeds up to 115 kilobits per second. Satellite communications in GHz bands are among the most rapidly growing new ICT media today. When the rate is fast enough to transfer an acceptable video-audio signal, it is usually described as a broadband channel (starting from 300 Kbps). Optical fibres with much higher frequencies provide broadband connectivity.

1.1.10. Information Objects

There are different types of information objects and their screen representations, including instruments to operate with them (editors), and then moves to more sophisticated tools.

1.1.10.1. Graphical user interface or GUI

Generally GUI allows you to use your eyes for information perception and your hands for actions over information objects. Direct manipulation of graphical objects on the screen in a way that allows you to see what is happening is referred to by the acronym WYSIWYG (What You See Is What You Get).

1.1.10.2. Desktop and window metaphor

In many computers, before dealing with any specific information object, you find the computer screen organised as a desktop. Several object names, called icons, lie on this desktop. You can move these and place them wherever you like. You can open an object, see its presentation (text or picture) on the screen, and work on it. Some of the objects are folders. Inside folders you find the names of other information objects—some of them are the names of other folders. Some of these are executable programs and you can start running them, usually with a graphical effect of the run seen in a window on the screen.

1.1.10.3. Texts

From the birth of the personal computer, working with texts has been the major application of ICT. Soon it initiated a new culture of writing since text on screen turned out to be much more flexible and transformable than written or typed text. The technology influenced the psychology and social context of writing, which, in turn, changed technology. Here is an example of how technology is changing the nature of text.

1.1.10.4. Video

Working with pre-recorded video-fragments, their cutting, sequencing in an arbitrary way, adding sound and special effects is now possible using ordinary personal computers. For children starting from an early age, this kind of video editing constitutes a powerful environment for their communicative development.

1.1.10.5. Timeline

A timeline of events can carry icons or pictograms, or other names linked to information objects representing events. In this way, a timeline is similar to time wall-charts. In these charts you can see the whole timeframe, with much more detail of events. The timeline can also be represented as moving in response to the cursor.

1.1.11. Two-dimensional Editing

Images on computer screens are combinations of pixels, and so the obvious way to construct or change an image is to create it pixel-by-pixel. To make this process simpler, we can use a magnifying glass tool. Of course, in most cases, this method takes too much time, but it can be used in special cases to make minor changes. More often we use corresponding methods of editing images by:

i) changing digitised photographic pictures, or

ii) making and changing different types of drawings.

1.1.11.1. Pictures

In the case of photographic images, the computer extends dramatically the set of tools and operations available: resizing, cropping, lightening, darkening, sharpening, and so on. In this way, photographs can be transformed quite professionally, and then combined in sophisticated ways.

1.1.11.2. Computer drawings

In computer drawing, there are two major options:

i) Using a brush tool or pen tool.

ii) Using additional software tools similar to a ruler, compass, and templates.

In the first option, software and hardware were developed to mimic traditional techniques and introduce new ones. The second option, the computer version of technical drawing, has developed enormously, especially in the field of Computer Aided Design (CAD).

1.1.11.3. Maps and multilayer images

One option with computer images is to have several layers for an image, which is helpful in an application such as editing maps. A special kind of graphical design is the production of plans and geographical maps. Today this is done mainly in so-called Geo-Information Systems (GIS). Maps produced with GIS are examples of multilayer images that can be edited in each layer separately. Good GIS has sophisticated mechanisms to represent objects like rivers, state borders, and place names on maps in order not to overlap.

1.1.12. Three-and Four-dimensional Editing

1.1.12.1. Computer aided design

Computer-Aided Design or CAD has replaced traditional drawing almost completely. CAD allows you to create a 3D object on the screen that you can then turn around in space. Like pre-computer design, CAD systems:

i) have developed in different directions, for use in architectural design, fashion design, machine construction (cars, aircraft), electronic design, and other fields; and
ii) use libraries of ready-made templates from particular professional fields, and multi-layer construction.

The so-called Computer-Aided Manufacturing (or CAM) is computerised design of the manufacturing process. CAD/CAM is a combination of two.

1.1.12.2. Computer animation

Sophisticated and expensive instruments as well as children's simple tool-kits can be used to create artistically impressive or scientifically precise and enlightening computer animations. More and more movie scenes are now produced in artificial settings with characters designed on a computer by means of special software. Students' animations are usually simple and two-dimensional (flat). Adding a time dimension makes them 3D objects. Simple animations made by groups of students over several hours can be more educative for the creators and more exiting for the spectators.

1.1.13. Multimedia Presentations

Tools are available to make and show sequences of static (still) screens of images. Screens can contain visual representations of various information objects: pictures, drawings, diagrams, tables, as well as important lines of text, visualisations of experimental data, and mathematical models. A sequence of screens constitutes a slide show. Such sequences can run autonomously, without a human operator, but are much more effective in association with live human speech. This is a so-called multimedia presentation.

Combinations of different kinds of output and different kinds of information objects are usually called multimedia. This term was coined in the early 1960s to denote the new synthetic genre of *avant-garde* artistic stage performances comprising action-painting, music, declamation, pantomime, slide-projections and dynamic colour lighting effects. In the 1970s, multimedia became the trade expression applied to joint enterprises in designing, producing, promoting and marketing best-selling books bundled with hit-movies of the same plot (or vice versa), accompanied by the film's music soundtrack, T-shirts emblasoned with portraits of starring actors, and other paraphernalia. The computer industry picked up this coinage in the mid-1980s and used it to describe hardware and software configurations able to run alphanumeric, graphic and sound processing sub-routines simultaneously. Of all technologies, computers are ideally suited to mixing or combining media.

1.1.13.1. Virtual reality and cyberspace

Cyberspace and virtual reality (VR) are perhaps the most frequently heard, and least defined, expressions of the digital era. Virtual reality was concocted as a commercial brand name for a line of advanced graphic video games in the early 1990s. Both coinages stuck and became household words in media and computer science. Cyberspace connotes an informational space that is generated inside each functioning computer and spreads outside toward a final confluence with other local cyberspaces in the emerging global web of interconnected computer networks. Virtual reality refers to the patterns of ongoing events in time and space that are perceived by our senses through visual, audible and tactile interfaces.

A VR is a computer world that tricks the senses or mind. A virtual glove might give you the feel of holding your hand in water or mud or honey. A VR cyber suit might make you feel as if you swam through water or mud or honey. VR grew out of cockpit simulators used to train pilots and may shape the home and office multimedia systems of the future. The idea of advanced VR systems as future substitutes for sex and drugs and classroom training is the stock and trade of modern science fiction or 'cyberpunk' writing.

Virtual reality has entered modern slang. Even contemporary anthropologists and philosophers use the term virtual realities (with no reference at all to digital technologies) to discuss dreams, myths, hallucinations and poetic fantasies, as well as a psychic fabric of scientific hypotheses, theoretical thinking, logical and mathematical reasoning, and other imaginative functions of the human mind. The shortest path to grasping the idea of computer-based virtual realities is to play a video game of car racing or, even better, war aircraft fighting, so popular among teenage boys. However, the use of simulated reality for learning purposes goes back at least to the 1960s, when professional flight simulators were introduced to train pilots and air craft controllers.

1.1.13.2. Hypertexts

Hypertexts are created in a more sophisticated manner, using a special computer language called HTML (Hypertext Mark-up Language) and special editors. A modern language to describe objects of all types is called XML. A language to create VR 3D objects permitting VR-actions and feedbacks is called VRML (Virtual Reality Markup Language). Three triggering mechanisms, supported by VRML, are:

i) Proximity—execution based on viewer position.
ii) Viewpoint—execute when selecting viewpoint.
iii) Touch—execute on viewer clicks.

1.1.13.3. Computers for special needs

A well-known phenomenon of living organisms, including humans, is compensation—the ability to substitute some if its functions and organs for lost ones. Computers and ICT are involved in the process of compensation in many ways. Computers can improve human senses, or substitute one for another. They can do even more, and operate different devices such as home appliances. Even for persons with the most severe challenges, the computer is a helpful tool with which to communicate and control the environment.

Visual disabilities can be compensated for with tactile or aural perception. Braille coding was invented long before computers, but Braille is a good example of discrete (in fact, binary) coding. It encodes any letter as a combination of dots in given positions, and so tactile reading and writing in Braille have been the form of written communication for blind people for years. Modern ICT have improved on Braille in straightforward and important ways. There is software to translate letters, digits, punctuation marks and other symbols into Braille codes; a special printer using special paper then can print these codes and other graphical images in relief form for a blind person. It is also possible to provide online reading: on a computer extension, pins corresponding to Braille dots pop up on a template line to form Braille letters. Alternative keyboards are also available for blind people, including ones especially designed for Braille (9-keys). They include a Braille line on which the typed text is displayed.

Keys of ordinary keyboards can be marked with Braille dot-letters as well. Another channel of perception for blind people is aural. Besides simple recording, computers can help to transform text into audible speech. In the simplest case, a computer reads aloud a sequential text, word-by-word. More advanced screen readers exploit structures beyond linear text, including hypertext. There are structures of text in programming languages and other professional environments that screen readers can navigate a blind person through.

For the non-blind, an aural channel can be used for input as well. In fact, full communication between user and computer can be based on verbal processes. A possible consequence of this is a decline in Braille literacy among the blind population, as there has been in other skills such as knowledge of multiplication tables since the advent of the calculator. The hearing-impaired can also be considerably supported by ICT in two major ways.

The first is the well-known amplification of incoming sonic signals. Unlike the old fashioned analogue hearing aid, digital devices can provide immensely wider customised choice and fine tuning of frequency equalisation versus loudness levels to help compensate for an individual's aural deficiencies.

The second aid is a speech visualiser for persons with more serious hearing losses. Invented in the early 1940s and named Visible Speech, this device analysed sound energy distribution of different speech formats, and displayed them as patterns of white, grey, and black patches on a monitor. The observer had the burden of guessing, interpreting, and deciding whether or not these images represented particular articulated syllables.

Today, the digital automated system converts spoken words into a typed text shown on the screen. In this way, even totally deaf people can converse through the telephone or in other situations where they cannot hear a speaker's words. For blinddeaf persons, the output signals of such systems may be fed into a digital Braille display to provide the same opportunity. In other areas, kinaesthetically (motor) impaired people can control their environment with the help of a computer and additional hardware. Text entry can be a major method of general communication for children (and adults) who have various types of problems including severe physical disabilities.

Children with cerebral palsy, for example, are able to communicate more easily by using bigger trackballs. There is a whole spectrum of new and emerging input devices, including some controlled by human breath only. At the same time, human adaptation can be high. For example, some people can type quite effectively on a standard keyboard with only one hand.

1.1.14. Software Tools

Software, the name given to the coded instructions that tell computers what to do, comes in many different forms. Here we focus on software tools that are useful for schools.

1.1.14.1. Operating systems

The software foundation of a computer system is called its operating system (OS). It is the environment with and through which other software communicates. OS with Graphical User Interface was developed by Apple and used in Macintosh computers. The most popular operating systems today are versions of the Windows system developed by Microsoft. In the 1980s, an operating system for larger computers called UNIX was created.

A version of UNIX that is popular and available for no cost today, even for less powerful personal computers, is Linux. The most popular application of computers today is text writing and editing, which extends to producing hypertexts and presenting internet pages, spreadsheets, and sending and receiving emails. These tools are often called office applications because they are widely used and effective in offices.

1.1.14.2. Professional tools

In most fields of human endeavour, specific applications have been developed with specific software tools. These collections of tools are called virtual workshops. In fact, you can call a collection of these instruments an editor of virtual reality. They can also be referred to as automated instruments, or electronic assistants of a human editor. Thus, in certain professional fields, we have specialised mathematical text editors, sound editors, database editors, and so on. CAD-systems, noted above, are used in different areas of design, including machine construction (for example, automotive and aircraft production), architectural design, book design, and microchip design. Naturally, specialised hardware can be required for CAD such as a more powerful CPU, monitors with higher resolution, graphical tablets, and plotters.

A special kind of design activity is the design of processes. Among these are:

a) computer-aided manufacturing (CAM), usually based on CAD design;
b) design of human activity in project planning and implementation; and
c) software design (also known as computer programming), one of the most sophisticated areas of human activity today.

1.1.14.3. Simulation

Simulations can be time-consuming: it might take a week, for example, to develop a really good simulation of the next day's weather. In some cases, however, we can shorten the process of simulation by using more sophisticated mathematical methods and algorithms. A system for simulating complex systems behaviour based on differential equations and graphical diagrams is called system dynamics and can be implemented with the help of a software environment (virtual lab) called Stella. In many cases, we may have a small piece of text (for example, the name of an information object) associated with two other pieces of text.

1.1.14.4. Control

Control is one of the most important real-life applications of ICT. Some of the processes of control are invisible, automatic, and do not assume ongoing human involvement. Others are interactive and assume the permanent participation of a human being in the system. In both cases, visualisation is important.

As we have seen, a great deal of information can be stored in a computer. A server, for example, with the capacity of a terabyte and costing a few thousand dollars can store the text of a million books, or about one thousand hours of video. Practically all the texts ever written could be stored in computers in one modest size building. Before long, one will be able to do the same with all art galleries, photo collections, and scanned archives of important documents, major speeches, music, and popular or artistically created movies. Nor is it necessary to have all this information in one place. The sources of information can be distributed all over the world and accessible via the internet.

Major efforts in these directions are being made in the form of electronic libraries, digital archives, libraries, and museums, and individual attempts. Some of these depositories are proprietary and closed for outsiders or require a subscription fee; but many are free to enter, open for the public, and can be used freely for educational purposes. In this context, two major problems arise: the quality of information and the accessibility of information. Neither problem is new. The first problem exists in the form of some tabloid newspapers or amateur writers.

Distributing information widely was expensive: it pays generally, for it to be accurate. The second problem is clearly seen in lost scientific and technological inventions, forgotten addresses and telephone numbers, and lost birth records. To deal with this problem, people invented libraries and archives, sophisticated forms of indexation and catalogues, review journals, citation indices, telephone directories, and all types of reference books, with their associated footnotes and references.

With the dawn of the internet age, these problems became more severe. The internet is full of poor information and hard-to-access or wasted information. To find needed information, you can spend hours and still not find what you want. For this reason, some say the internet is useless, even destructive and dangerous. In overcoming these difficulties, the world ICT community has invented many mechanisms.

A major opportunity provided by modern ICT is the ability to gather in a single computer information contained in millions of volumes contained in other computers. By using the mouse to click on a word on the computer screen, you can immediately call up (possibly, in a different window) a piece of information referred to by the author of the initial text who provided the link or reference. Catalogues and reference libraries of internet resources have been developed and placed on the internet by institutions and individuals.

ICT are ideal for making catalogues but descriptions need to be added. In the past few years, major attempts have been made in this direction by establishing standards of so-called metadata.

Standards : Another dimension is standards for storing data like texts and images. There was a time when you bought a new computer and a new text editor only to find that you could not read your old files. Therefore, a strong trend is to have a system of standards that are free, open, written in understandable form, and which describe how data are stored and displayed on screen.

Reusability : Many information objects are present as parts of other objects. An immediate example is a painting in a museum collection. For obvious reasons, especially in education, we would like the opportunity to access such an individual object independently. Technically it is easy, but serious organisational and copyright problems await solution.

Search engines: Major attempts are being made to keep track of all internet information resources. This tracking can be based on an analysis of word content. Thus, you can ask a search engine to show all references to a word, or word-phrase, over the entire internet. More sophisticated searches can be done using more complex inquiries, for instance, containing a certain combination of words, together with a particular word, but perhaps not containing some other word.

Portals: Search engines are approximate search methods, and they do not evaluate the quality of any information found. Another approach, combined with the search engine approach, consists of evaluating and describing internet resources by particular organisations or professional associations to ensure quality of the resources as well as quality of the search, and to gather all this information in a single location, called a portal.

Safety systems : The mechanisms noted above do not limit access to the internet by any computer. At the same time, there is increasing concern among parents and teachers over the dangerous influence of the internet on the younger generation. Pornography, hate, violence, and narcotics are often targeted specifically at young people. Concerned citizens are therefore seeking to form a barrier against this influence—an internet safety infrastructure. Parents or a school can subscribe to a safety service, and all access to the internet will go through this infrastructure, which does not permit the user to go to proscribed websites.

In fact, there is a lot of free information on the internet. Several countries have launched free electronic archives, and digitised their cultural heritage. The idea of open and free information space is at once popular but also disturbing, not only among educators, but among software developers as well.

Many software products in schools are open and allow:

i) teachers and students to use data and images for their personal use;

ii) students to create experiments in virtual labs, and teachers to create tests; and

iii) students to store their work for a period of study in a unified information space open to other students and teachers, parents and other schools.

References

Anderson, J., "The New Literacy and Technology", *Keynote address to the International Reading Association Convention*, San Antonio, Texas, April 1993.

Farnham-Diggory, S., *Schooling*, Harvard University Press, Cambridge, MA., 1990.

Friedhoff, R. and Benzon, W., "Visualisation: The Second Computer Revolution", Harry N. Abrams, New York, 1989.

Gardner, H., *Frames of Mind: The Theory of Multiple Intelligences*, Basic Books, New York, 1983.

Heineke, W.F. and Blasi, L. (Eds)., *Methods of Evaluating Educational Technology*, Information Age Publishing, Greenwich, Connecticut, 2001.

Mumford, L., *The Myth of The Machine: Technics and Human Development*, Harcourt, Brace and World, New York, 1967.

Papert, S., *Mindstorms: Children, Computers, and Powerful Ideas*, Basic Books, New York, 1981.

Krishnamurthy R.C., *Network-based Teaching and Learning*, Authorspress, New Delhi, 2004.

Sternberg, R.J., *The Triarchic Mind: A New Theory of Intelligence*, Viking Press, New York, 1988.

UNESCO, *Information and Communication Technologies in Teacher Education: A Planning Guide* (Ed. P. Resta), UNESCO, Paris, 2002.

UNESCO, *Information and Communication Technologies in Schools, A Handbook for Teachers*, 2005.

2

Schools in Transition

The teacher is always in search of a learner, and vice versa. When there is no learner in sight, teachers will try to awake, or invoke the will to learn in anyone they happen to meet. The teacher does this by challenging the other person's curiosity, ambition, inquisitiveness, or just playfulness with any means at hand. A learner is also always in search of a teacher. Where there is no teacher available, learners will recruit anyone they meet as a possible teacher. If there is no one at all, they will figure out a kind of virtual substitute teacher inside their own soul. The three facets of any educational event:

i) encounter,

ii) communication and

iii) interaction.

Encounters are face-to-face meetings; situations when you find yourself faced by other individuals and feel prompted to relate somehow to their presence.

Communication is an exchange of messages, sent and received by at least two people, expressing their feelings, thoughts and intentions to each other in the hope for reciprocity.

Interactions are processes where two, or more actors influence and affect each other's actions and behaviour while striving to reach their goals, doing some common work, or performing a joint task.

Any interaction, by definition, generates information. Not all information generated by an interaction needs to be communicated; some parts of this information may be intentionally concealed. One actor may purposely search for, uncover, and collect the information that another actor tries to conceal. At times it is difficult to draw a strict line between communication and interaction. For example, if during language classes, a teacher uses verbal means to enact modes of argumentation for students, communication and interaction become one and the same.

2.1. Human Information Activities in Learning

For centuries, communication between human beings has been carried out in oral and written form. Oral communication goes through the aural channel of information, more often than not supported by the visual channel (a speaker's movements and everything else that constitutes theatrical aspects of communication). Oral communication used to be immediate until recent centuries when it became possible to have it recorded. It was an interesting moment in human history, when the recording of dynamic images of communication was invented and developed, before the recording of dynamic sound was possible.

This was the era of the Great Mute (as they used to call the cinematograph until it was coupled with recorded sound), where moving pictures on the screen were accompanied by subtitles (and live music) only. Communication can go in one direction as in radio and TV broadcasting, or in two directions as in oral discussions or telephone conversation. Written communication goes through a visual channel, where text is supported by pictorial illustrations. All these models and modes are presented in learning and teaching, and all have been, and are being, radically changed by ICT.

Learning can involve also doing something in the physical world, particularly, making objects. This includes making messages, which, in this respect, intersects with the communication process, though the accent in the doing is made on constructing the message, not delivering it. Therefore, cases of doing in learning are represented by constructing:

i) an information object (an actual or potential message),
ii) an information process (composing and editing),
iii) a mental, inner object (reasoning and imagining), and
iv) a material object or process.

These activities, while being in many aspects interrelated, can be efficiently supported by different uses of ICT.

2.1.1. Observation

Observation is another process involved in learning. The learner is an active participant in the game here. A further important element in the formation of a thinking human being is reflection—the process and the ability to observe yourself and your activity from the outside. An ancient and powerful tool for reflection is a mirror. Observing another human in order to copy, imitate, and do the same, is another important model of learning. The modern type of mirror that keeps track of disappearing images is a video-recorder.

2.1.2. Searching for Information

Searching for information was not a popular activity in traditional schooling but has become more and more important in modern life. Previously, if any searching was done, it was primarily in a person's memory. People were considered intelligent, knowledgeable, and wise if they could output quickly the needed information from memory. Even then, books (of wisdom) were occasionally used to answer a question, but the books were not considered as an everyday source of information with the exception, perhaps, of medical doctors and lawyers.

Today the search and retrieval of needed information is becoming a core activity in work and learning. Asking an expert is a special case of information search. As with information searches, questioning is becoming more and more important in the information age. Receiving aural and visual information in studying a school subject is a prerequisite, but it is just the first step to assimilating its content.

True learning occurs only in an intensive conversation between teacher and student, as well as between students, as all good pedagogues since the days of Socrates have known. What a pity that this principle was forgotten, or neglected by those teachers in many 20th century-era schools who thought they were there to teach, not to converse.

2.1.3. Contradictory Demands in Schooling

Contemporary education is replete with contradictory demands. The educational system of the 21st century must be oriented toward creating conditions that allow school students to act and learn freely in productive collaboration with their teachers, and also with their parents and other members of their community, local and global. In this, the application of ICT appears to be a necessity, as well as a pledge of success.

School-related activities can be broadly divided into two categories—internal and external—that the school as an organisation is called upon to sustain. Internal activities are carried out within the school's scheduled hours and inside the school walls. These core, central, obligatory and strictly formalised activities—one is tempted to say almost sacred activities—are the school's classes or lessons, comprising teaching and learning. Activities during intermissions are profane, and activities after scheduled hours are a mixture of the two. There are also internal activities of administration and supervision, and teachers' meetings, which are conducted without the involvement of students. All these activities imply an exchange of information, carried out through a number of channels, some established, officially approved, and highly formalised; the others, informal, weakly delineated, not always approved, often rebuked and prohibited, and thus covert, and even kept in strict secrecy.

External learning activities, besides sports and clubs, are mainly homework. Students do their homework in an isolated, individual manner. The relation to internal activity is often through short assignment notes. Consultations with teachers, discussions with peers are occasional and irregular, as is cooperative work. External activities of school administrators are working meetings and consulting with superiors and colleagues from other schools, seminars, training sessions, and conferences.

Organisational aspect of schooling should be neglected in relation to the use of ICT. One of the greatest errors in education is to assume that the larger social context of the school is irrelevant or even secondary to learning. The social structure of the school is not simply the context of learning; it is part of what is learned. High school, therefore, is not simply a bad experience for these students—it teaches them lessons that threaten to limit them for the rest of their lives. Writing about business organisations, rather than schools, managerial scientists often refer to learning organisations.

Since at the present rate of technological change the problems to be solved differ from one day to the next, it follows that everybody in the organisation, from those who frame the policies to those who manipulate the ultimate details of technique, must be endowed to the possible extent with the means of learning. The school can evolve and change its structure and functions in response to the new challenges.

2.2. School: A Social Organisation

An outstanding historian-philosopher of technology, Lewis Mumford, described the new kind of religious, socio-political, industrial and military organisation, invented during the Bronze Age under the aegis of the priest-kings, as a megamachine. Being essentially coercive, undemocratic and hierarchical, such an organisation paved the way to, and was inherited by, succeeding civilisations. Only recently was it questioned and challenged by a new vision of human progress based on other principles.

Through this millennial old legacy, the school appears to be the social organisation most resistant to change. In fact, it mostly strives to keep its basic structures and functions unchanged, including its information circuits, channels, and routes. There was no serious lack of quality as long as education remained a heavily guarded treasure or luxury, accessible only to a chosen few. Formal schooling was reserved exclusively for the high priesthood and aristocratic families, and denied to anyone outside the cloisters and castle walls.

The minds of pre-schoolers were considered a plain tablet or a blank sheet of paper upon which teachers could write anything they, or some higher authority, would think appropriate. In a short while, the thinking about what was appropriate to teach children was taken away from teachers and concentrated in the hands of those in political and economic power. No less significant technologically and educationally was Gutenberg's concept of setting up a line of type by using separate letters cast in a uniform pattern in a mould: the origin of the standardised, replaceable part of ever increasingly automated machinery.

It was only logical to apply the same principles to schooling, and since the mid-nineteenth century, this approach has prevailed in most Western countries. A system was established where children and young people could learn different subjects from different teachers who, in their turn, could rely safely on a standard, ready-made curriculum and procedures designed by other specialists.

The centralised pedagogical research institutions that design the curricula, instructional methods, textbooks and other materials, which, after having a stamp of approval from ministries of education, are distributed to schools and teachers. A teacher's duty is to read and follow closely the body of these materials in order to deliver it piecemeal to students, who are expected to memorise the content one chunk after another, and checking in to see if they succeed. The basic, though rarely announced, assumption is that teachers need not add a word to what has been given from higher authorities.

A principal and a supervisor receive from the higher educational authorities an approved bundle of curriculum-and-procedure materials and distribute these different packages among the teachers of particular disciplines. Each teacher subdivides the received package in accordance with the age grouping of students, the quotas of curriculum content to be assimilated daily, and the school timetable. Teacher-to-student communication is predominantly oral. There is little hands-on activity with physical materials and tools on workbenches. The teacher is a lecturer, not a master of a craft (menial or mental).

Little communication exists between teachers of different subjects on how to collaborate in making the educational process truly involving and exiting. Teachers and learners do in the traditional classroom of the old school:

i) *Teachers speak, learners listen.* Teachers talk to learners, who listen to and supposedly perceive, understand and memorise what is said. Often, this is all that teachers do on a strictly formal, technical-operational plane.

ii) Teachers write letters, numbers, words and phrases on the chalkboard to help students hold facts in their short- and long-term memories.

iii) Teachers paste (clip) to the chalkboard, or hang on the wall, posters with pre-written (printed) letters, words and numbers, and then point to them with their finger or a pointer while giving explications, explanations and instructions.

iv) Teachers draw or use ready-made diagrams or images of certain objects or scenes related in some way to what they are saying.

v) Teachers bring three-dimensional objects to illustrate lessons.

Teachers manipulate these 3-D objects (other than to point to them or take them in their hands to show them to the class) in a transformative way, for example by using them in applied functions they are meant to illustrate. To show such manipulations and transformations of 3-D objects, teachers use workbenches.

Teachers conduct spectacular experiments that excite students and which they remember all their lives. In short, notwithstanding the content, the main tool and carrier of the teacher's message is the word, or, more precisely, the oral and, to a lesser degree, written speech. In such classrooms, learners are not required or expected to:

a) do anything besides follow a teacher's presentations and instructions expressed in oral and written words (texts) until they can assimilate and reproduce verbally the knowledge and skills required; draw in language or mathematics workbooks except perhaps for geometry, or drawing primitive diagrams for science;

b) manipulate or transform three-dimensional objects, other than, perhaps, paper, scissors, glue and pencils.

c) discover, invent, design, and construct during classes anything of their own in relation to the curricular content; or

d) converse with classmates on the content being taught.

In a scheduled class period, the teacher delivers the assigned chunk of information simultaneously to all students in a monologue broadcast type of lecture. While taking in information coming from the teacher, students are obliged to remain silent and motionless until the teacher stops the delivery and asks them if everybody has clearly understood what was said. Then those who may not have understood can raise their hands and, after being granted the right to speak, say what escaped their comprehension.

Teachers repeat an explanation twice or even three times, but often there is no time to clarify all problems, and there are always one or more students who dare not express their difficulties. Common sense prompts one to think that those who are in need might seek and find some help from their nearest neighbours in the classroom. Sadly, more often than not, such a common sense approach does not happen in classical schooling. As everybody knows, communication between students during classes is usually frowned upon because it threatens to disrupt the very foundation of classical teaching.

Information is constantly filtered downwards through the hierarchical system and no horizontal roots are stipulated. When a teacher gives a class an assignment demanding writing, calculating, or reasoning, each student is supposed to do the task individually and by themselves. No consultation with classmates is allowed, and any breaking of this rule is often punished. Consequently, nothing even remotely resembling collaboration, productive discussion and teamwork is practised; neither are the corresponding skills being developed. As a result (and this becomes evident after some testing questions made by the teacher), not all students receive the full amount of curriculum information supposedly transmitted to them during class periods.

Students do not have the channels, and nor are they encouraged, to exchange views and opinions about the curriculum. It is not surprising then that very few of them are motivated enough to discuss such things out of classes except to complain about it. Anyway, such behaviour is not anticipated or wanted in traditional curricula and procedures. In such circumstances, one might conclude that most traditional school authorities would readily reject the idea of adopting ICT that would enable students to sustain autonomous information exchanges during classes.

Due to society's evolving expectations of equal educational opportunity for all and the current emphasis on relevant and quality opportunity for all, the school system has developed into an increasingly complex organisational structure. This structure requires extensive and comprehensive administration and has enough problems sustaining stable and malleable conditions to put aside the problems of its transformative development. That is, to sustain the conditions that give teachers and administrators intellectual and emotional comfort, they naturally tend to see schools as exclusively teaching institutions.

The sum of what must be taught and learned, despite the charge to have it integrated and holistic, remains a collection of disjointed, isolated and unrelated subjects, struggling for allocated hours in the school timetable. No evident connection exists between corresponding activities or between actors (functional agents); no channels through which they can communicate and talk to each other; and no space for their mutual encounter and subsequent interaction.

Quite naturally, there is little information exchange between them precisely because subject matter in the classical school curriculum is impersonal, faceless and soulless.

Neither teachers nor students can feel and see in such classrooms other living, willing, and acting personalities—those bearers of creative forces that had once brought into being all these areas of knowledge, mastery and expertise. No wonder they have little motivation to explore and develop the hidden inner potential of their own.

2.2.1. Detechnicalised Learning

The mechanical-industrial syndrome is still felt in many areas of education, especially among the administrative staff. The vision of a smoothly run manufacturing plant with its driving belts and assembly lines does often eclipse the fact that school is (or at least, is said to be) a living entity, a society in miniature, a learning community of people, comprising some adults but mostly children drawn and bound together by extreme variegated needs, expectations, obligations, and responsibilities.

In fact, institutionalised, compulsory education was turned into a machine (a mechanical production system), imparting its products with an inner programme to proliferate the same pattern in all walks of life. Hence, the school became the model for the mechanisation of society. Increasingly fragmented division of labour and specialisation were, and still are, the key words. In fact, it was a cycle (or vicious circle) of mutual reinforcement that reached a climax in the mid-twentieth century. At the beginning of the new millennium, this cycle came to a dead-end.

2.3. Possibilities of New Pedagogy

Proposals for a radical reformation of traditional schooling are numerous. Dictionaries define intelligence as the power of seeing, learning, understanding and knowing. It is a mental ability. Intelligence has been equated with the ability to think rationally and objectively, and to express one's thoughts and judgments in scientifically based, quantitatively measurable, logically provable propositions and assertions. Individuals were called intelligent if they were astute, shrewd, eloquent and quick in using words and numbers, especially in written form.

Consequently, teaching and learning in Western schools were more concerned with transmitting and getting detachable and distant knowledge coded symbolically in oral and written speech, rather than with immediate interaction and participatory hands-on activities, experience and wisdom. It was quite natural to establish a system of checking and testing both interim results and the quality of the end-products of this almost industrial-like manufacturing process.

In pre-industrial epochs, people perceived each other as much more complex entities. Someone could be clever enough with words while incompetent in numbers; shrewd in business but poor in writing; incapable in abstract reasoning but masterful in crafts or apt in sports. It was only after the development of intelligence tests and what the statistician Spearman did with them that the construct of intelligence nested so firmly in the consciousness of educators and heads of Human Resource departments. Eventually, all these tests, rather than measuring potential for achievement became the measure of achievement. More to the point, the tests that had been designed to sample education now came to determine what was taught. In the 1980s, Howard Gardner formulated his theory of multiple intelligences, in which he stated that people use one or more of at least seven (more recently eight and even nine) relatively autonomous, intellectual capacities to approach problems and create products. In many aspects, Gardner's views run against entrenched notions of pedagogical psychology.

Gardner's seven intelligencies are:

i) Linguistic intelligence (as in a poet);

ii) Logical-mathematical intelligence (as in a scientist);

iii) Musical intelligence (as in a composer);

iv) Spatial intelligence (as in a sculptor or flight pilot);

v) Bodily kinaesthetic intelligence (as in an athlete or dancer);

vi) Interpersonal intelligence (as in a salesman or teacher);

viii) Intrapersonal intelligence (exhibited by individuals with accurate views of themselves).

The time has come for schools to incorporate a wider array of mental processes and activities into the learning process. Whereas traditional classes have been dominated by the spoken and printed word, the new classroom should practise a multisensory enhanced learning. Intelligence is always an interaction between biological proclivities and opportunities for learning in a particular cultural context.

For everyone, developing these multiple intelligences increases creativity, flexibility of thinking, and the broad cultural and humanitarian background that enriches living. The resources for this enrichment are typically thought of as material artifacts like books, textbooks, and computer files. However, other individuals are part of one's distributed intelligence also. Most workers do not depend exclusively on their own skills and understanding; rather, they assume the presence of others in their work environments.

Another approach to the nature, structure and functions of intelligence(s) has been proposed by Robert Sternberg, who suggests three kinds of intelligence:

i) componential, which is assessed by many traditional tests used today;

ii) contextual, which is the source of creative insight, and

iii) experiential, which is the street smarts of intelligence.

Sternberg's latter two intelligences do not often show up on traditional tests, and are not always highly valued in the classroom, since curious and creative students and those who learn by doing tend to take up more of a teacher's time and attention. Such students are later valued in the adult world, however, as creative thinkers and process-oriented employees who often affect the bottom line in productive ways.

Sternberg feels that some people's major intelligence is in the traditionally tested/graded area of critical thinking (generating new innovative thought and connection), and that people who are able to make things really work for them out there in real life are contextual thinkers. Sternberg's theory is too complex to be elaborated here in full detail. One of its outcomes is the Sternberg Triarchic Abilities Test (STAT), which is divided into nine multiple levels for different ages, and described as suitable for kindergarten through college, as well as for adults. In contrast to conventional tests, STAT yields separate scores for componential information processing (analytical ability), coping with novelty (synthetic ability), and (as a separate score) automatisation and practical-intellectual skills.

Equally important, the test puts more emphasis on the ability to learn than on what has been learned, and verbal skill is measured by learning from context, not by vocabulary. The test also measures skills for coping with novelty, whereby the examinee must imagine a hypothetical state of the world (such as cats being magnetic) and then reason as though this state of the world were true. In yet another example, STAT measures practical abilities such as reasoning about advertisements and political slogans, not just decontextualised words or geometric forms.

In fact, as Sternberg himself admits, STAT is not immune to prior learning, and nor is it culture-free. It is hardly thinkable to design a test that would satisfy all the considered demands. Intelligence is always used in some particular, usually rather restricted context, though it is highly desirable to have this context as wide as possible. Sternberg's theory differs from Gardner's. However, the two theories are also highly complementary. Sternberg believe that intelligence needs to be seen as a broader and more complex construct than both authors declare, and the field is open to any experienced, thoughtful, and enterprising teacher eager to make her or his own contribution to the common educational cauldron.

Children have a natural interest and curiosity about the internal and external world, and an eagerness to communicate and to play, making collections and ordering items, creating unexpected and aesthetically significant objects. The basis for human development—habits and skills for lifelong learning should be established early in primary schools.

The objective, sterile environment in many schools actually inhibits learning. Learning is also unlikely to occur when students harbour negative feelings about an instructor, peers, class work, or have difficult personal issues. The traditional classroom must be replaced by rich, stimulating, accepting, warm, and responsive surroundings. Both children and adults acquire knowledge from active participation in holistic, complex, meaningful environments organised around longterm goals. Fractionated instruction maximises forgetting, inattention, and passivity. Today's school programmes could hardly have been better designed to prevent a child's natural learning system from operating.

As most teachers know, students labeled weak or slow often turn out to be bright and skilful when confronted with something that is personally appealing or challenging outside the classroom. Though these students have difficulty learning in school, they often excel at making, fixing and operating tangible things: gadgets, bicycles, motors, electrical circuits, complex mechanical devices, arcade games, VCRs, various kinds of contraptions and even imaginary objects. These children are usually identified as having trouble with the symbolic smarts that form the core of schooling.

It is not surprising that the traditional school focuses on what weak students cannot do, and does not see them as possessing virtuoso sensory smarts in some fields. Instead, it sees them as failing to perform, or not meeting the requirements. An ideal teacher will appeal equally to symbolic and sensory smart students with a view to bringing these two kinds of knowledge into active and fruitful collaboration. When students are encouraged by teachers to reflect on and confront the differences and similarities that emerge as they move across materials, sensory modalities, and kinds of descriptions, it helps them to create mental bridges between action knowledge and symbolic knowledge.

Children who build both real world and virtual world structures begin to see the resemblance among working systems. In making the resemblance explicit, they liberate and make easily understandable the basic principles that the working systems share.

2.3.1. Visualisation

Visualisation of inner mental imagery and the outer graphic presentation of reality in pictures, drawings, diagrams, lists, and charts is a fundamental part of creativity, discovery, invention, and problem solving. The vital importance of visualisation is affirmed by the fact that a surprisingly large proportion of the human cortex is devoted to vision and visual analysis, and that the bandwidth of the visual channel is greater than that of any other sense. In many instances, the eye, and those parts of the brain that process visual information, lay the foundation for enhancing conscious thinking, which in turn, grows from our preconscious mental activity. To take full advantage of the capabilities of the eye, the goal of visualisation should be objectification. This means that a phenomenon, inherently visual or not, should be represented as having form, colour, texture, motion and other qualities of objects.

Inductive thinking relies to a great extent upon the human ability to visualise on this preconscious level. Major portions of the visual system including the retina, the structures ascending to the visual cortex, and parts of the visual cortex itself fall into the preconscious category. More powerful than a supercomputer, these functional entities relentlessly perform information-processing miracles, creating a three-dimensional, coloured visual environment that our conscious self exploits in a logical way to serve definite practical purposes.

The conceptual images are constantly being analysed at a preconscious level, and produce useful data for establishing spatial relations, making conscious representations and building plans. In other words, the outcomes of these subliminal mental activities become the elements, tools, and procedures of rational thinking. This is where computers make an enormous difference. When we visualise with the help of computers, video camcorders, and big-screen high-resolution projection, we restructure a problem situation so that more of it can be processed by the preconscious part of our brain—the visual system that is our silent partner. In this way, consciousness can be devoted to higher levels of critical analysis and synthesis. Especially interesting, are virtual worlds that model nothing but themselves, as do many games, chess among them.

Nevertheless, by representing spatially the system of abstract relations between chessmen on a chessboard, a professional chess player can think in images. Similarly, it is also possible to visualise on a computer screen the spatial interrelations of elementary predicates and, consequently, to represent complex formulas of predicate logic. As a kind of modelling, visualisation has many aspects. One is aestheticemotional. For example, nobody will deny that visualised mathematical objects and functions can be aesthetically beautiful. Fractal animated cartoons, captivatingly spectacular and shown on TV all over the world, have already inspired works of fine art (even if not eternal masterpieces). Beyond any doubt, it is precisely because of their aesthetic components that such themes as chaos, fractals, and the like, have become so popular in academic mathematical courses.

Another aspect of visualisation-as-modelling is, as in the classical art of painting, selecting and making visible essential traits of the object or phenomenon depicted. By forcing us to pay attention only to what can be seen and perceived by the eye, visualising helps to impart a meaning to a problem and makes it easier to find its solution. In the simplest case of a virtual constructor used to build interactive models of physical phenomena. Using a similar learning environment under a teacher's guidance, the student can trace all levels of abstractions in modelling. For instance, there could be genuine physical objects and processes (say, a carousel on which children have a ride), material models, videotapes, computer simulations (virtual realities), graphical representations of processes' characteristics by co-ordinates and velocities within a set referential system, and symbolic modelling by algebraic and differential equations.

New pedagogy is based on the opposite of the traditional classical hierarchy -that is, a heterarchy, a term that depicts a system in which each working element or agent is equally ruled by all others. This means that, while learning, these agents communicate or talk to each other, exchanging messages filled with related information. In this system, there are no simple linear chains of cause and effect, but more and more cross-connected rings and loops. Behind the dazzling variety of new theories, methodologies, and working approaches to learning, one can detect several underlying patterns, or fundamental principles and practices that seem perennial. Re-christened in modern idioms, these principles are referred to as poly-sensory, experiential, project-oriented, constructivist, and connectionist.

2.3.2. Constructivism

Jean Piaget, who introduced the term Constructivism, asserts that the knowledge acquired by students should not be supplied by the teacher as a ready-made product. Children do best by creating for themselves the specific knowledge they need, rather than being instructed in what they must know. Seymour Papert later found that such things would happen especially felicitously when learners are engaged in constructing something external or at least shareable: a sand castle, a book, a machine, a computer programme. These kinds of activities lead to a model of learning that involves a cycle of internalisation of what is outside, then externalisation of what is inside, and so on.

2.3.3. Connectivism

This mode of collaboration paves the way to connectivism, or connectionism or connectivity of knowledge, which Seymour Papert professed after many years clinging to logical step-by-step constructivism. The deliberate part of learning consists of making connections between mental entities that already exist; new mental entities seem to come into existence in more subtle ways that escape conscious (i.e., step-by-step) control. This offers a strategy to facilitate learning by improving the connectivity in the learning environment, by actions on cultures rather than on individuals. Papert asserts that conceptual connections between a given notion or phenomenon and a wide array of other notions and phenomena are often helpful in gaining a more substantial understanding of a subject under study.

Rather than passively receiving ready-made facts, notions and opinions, students acquire advanced skills and knowledge by solving problems in their immediate surroundings that they consider personally meaningful and emotionally exciting. In the days of sweeping global changes, training for a particular skill or job must endow the trainee with an ability to be re-trained and self-retrained. Constructivist education must take command even in vocational and elementary schools, and a trainee must become a true learner. The priority is not the trans-mission of particular knowledge and skills from teacher to taught, but the development of the ability to acquire these by students on their own. All this, of course, is facilitated by new technologies of education.

For many decades, the polemics surrounding educational reform have vacillated between two points of view: those who favour a progressive, child-centred form of education, and those who prefer a return to a more structured, teacher directed curriculum that emphasises basic knowledge and skills. Today, however, a growing number of educators adhere to an alternative trend, intended to reconcile these opposing stances. This latter view is the theory of a collaborative community of teacher and students, focused on a dialogue and co-construction of knowledge. Such an approach helps resolve the conflict between traditional instructive teaching and constructive-connectivist autonomous learning. In this, too, ICT are playing a key role.

School teachers must revise their positions, leaving behind the status of the omniscient one who has all the answers. Instead, genuine teachers will become advisers and learning facilitators. Influence and credibility will accrue to those who not only instruct but also construct and connect in front of the class, that is, by skillfully doing something they may really be interested in, prompting students to learn how to do it by their own minds and hands.

Possible learning projects are as diverse as assembling and operating model cars and toy trains, building and decorating puppet homes, writing and printing prose and poetry via a word processor and desktop publishing, turning out pop tunes with a synthesiser, drawing simple animated cartoons, or cracking the codes of mediocre computer games in order to make them more challenging. The main goal of this construction and connection should be, of course, the acquisition of knowledge and skills required by the curriculum, plus the experience of being in control of one's own process of collaborative teaching and learning.

References

Gardner, H., *The Unschooled Mind: How children think and how schools should teach*, Basic Books, New York, 1991.

Talesra, Hemlata, Shukul and Sharma, *Challenges of Education: Technology, Trends, Globalisation*, Authorspress, 2003.

Perelman, L.J., *School's Out: Hyperlearning, The New Technology, and the End of Education*, William Morrow and Company, New York, 1992.

UNESCO, *Information and Communication Technology in Education: A Curriculum for Schools and Programme of Teacher Development* (Eds. J. Anderson and T. van Weert), 2002.

UNESCO, *Information and Communication Technologies in Schools, A Handbook for Teachers*, 2005.

3

Technology Access in Schools

Computer and educational technologies do indeed have the potential for bringing the world's resources to each and every child, privileged and underprivileged, tying parents directly to teachers, replacing rote learning with exciting interactive study, and cutting administrative costs. These technologies can serve to facilitate sweeping, democratic social changes.

Schools and universities have been wired, rewired, and fitted with state-of-the art educational technologies, as well as the accompanying computer hardware and software packages, only to be told in as little as six months to two years later that their initial investment is now obsolete. Accessibility to educational technologies serve as a mechanism of empowerment and enhanced social mobility for children attending schools within high-poverty.

Socio-historical inequalities appear to condition and be conditioned by new socio-economic and socio-political developments in both democratic and non-democratic societies alike. Likewise, over the past two decades, computers and their attendant technologies have increasingly conditioned the society in which we live, radically altering the way we organise, perceive, and interpret their worlds. Certainly, within the past decade, we have fundamentally reshaped and transformed our own culture and our own way of life by creating an epoch, in which we currently live, called the information age.

Nevertheless, inasmuch as computer and information technologies hold promise for improving individuals' lives in an information-driven twenty-first century, computers and their technological applications also have the power to reshape and reproduce systematically the same socio-historical and structural inequalities that have always existed in society. That is, computer technologies—and the attendant fallacy that there is immediate, equitable, and widespread adoption of and access to computers by all members of society—actually have the potential to perpetuate the same socio-historical and structural disparities along traditional and all-too-familiar lines of social inequity—namely, those of class advantage and racial bias.

In virtually every society at the beginning of the twenty-first century, polarities of income, class, race, ethnicity, national origin, gender, disability, and geographical space (e.g., locale and type of residence) are translating into ever widening and inequitable social gaps throughout every society. Regrettably, the role computers and their attendant technologies play in the amplification and magnification of these disparities has come to be known as the "digital divide".

The digital divide reveals itself within the context of several salient issues, one of which is accessibility: accessibility to computers and to the internet, accessibility to educational and information technologies, and accessibility to the skill training necessary for adequate computer literacy and technological fluency. More specifically, there are three sub-dimensions:

i) possession of the financial capital by which to purchase home computers and internet access;
ii) ability to generate a substantive tax base for neighborhood public schools and school districts to afford implementation of classroom informational and educational technologies; and
iii) possession of the necessary technical skills to be able to use computers, the internet, and to demonstrate adequate computer proficiency.

With the expanding implementation of educational technologies into the classrooms since the 1980s, computer literacy and technological fluency have increasingly become the definitive benchmarks as ports of entry into an increasingly meritocratic and technologically-oriented labor force, underscored by a commodification of information-based services and intellectual technologies. Social ascendancy and social mobility will be increasingly defined in terms of whether or not one possesses adequate and requisite computer literacy skills.

Since emerging educational trends oftentimes follow and/or concurrently develop in response to larger economic trends, the development and implementation of course curricula and pedagogical strategies also frequently attempt to emulate shifting socio-economic developments, especially within the labour force. In other words, depending on the socio-economic trends occurring within a given socio-historical point in time, the classroom becomes the proving ground for training and eventual participation in the labour force.

The provision of curricula designed to generate digital literacy and technological fluency among today's elementary, secondary, and post-secondary students may come to service only those students whose parents reside in school districts with an affluent tax base that can financially subsidize a digital public education. For the post-secondary student, the price of a digital education may be too difficult to afford or for their parents to finance. In other words, the price of a digital education is steep—an expense that many individuals and school districts may simply not be able (or choose not) to afford.

Differences in degrees of digital and technological expertise, therefore, will emerge between students who benefit from their parents residing in affluent tax base school districts as opposed to students whose parents live in less affluent tax base or high poverty school districts.

If a democratic society believes that there is a strong relationship between accessibility to a publicly financed education and increasing the citizenry's hope to minimise social inequalities, increase social justice within society, expand job opportunities, and enhance their accessibility to improved social mobility through education, then education—and in these days, a digital education—can indeed become the mechanism for social empowerment by which to leverage upward social mobility.

However, if computer-aided, educational technologies do more to discourage a citizenry's belief in the attainment of true democratic ideals because equality of opportunity for a fair and equitable, publicly financed, and increasingly digitised education is absent, then the hope for greater equality and social justice, increased job opportunity, and enhanced accessibility to improved social mobility will indeed dim.

As students graduate from elementary and secondary schools and attempt to move toward the achievement of a post-secondary education and eventual participation in the post-industrial work force, those with digital deficits may be less likely to achieve levels of social mobility and social ascendancy that their more digitally proficient counterparts are likely to attain. The former are more likely to require remediation of their digital deficits at the post-secondary level of education or have become so discouraged and feel so disempowered by their elementary and secondary digital educational experiences that they take jobs that require little to no computer literacy skills.

Today, as admission to post-secondary educational institutions becomes increasingly competitive, some institutions are now placing the onus on the student applicant to be fairly computer literate or technologically proficient. Although not part of the formal application and admission processes yet, there may come a day in the not-too-distant future when technological and computer literacy will become as much a requirement for college admission as are three to four years of high school mathematics and English. In other words, formal college admission may become contingent upon a computer skills repertoire of ample depth and breadth.

For underprivileged elementary and secondary students, coming from less than adequate digital educational backgrounds and possessing digital deficits in their computer literacy, a college admission that becomes contingent upon possession of adequate computer literacy skills will become one more of the many social inequality barriers that are all but easily conquered on the historically underprivileged student's social mobility ladder. Thus, the historically underprivileged student's barrier to social mobility becomes the pivotal stepping stone on the path to accessing "the keys to the kingdom" for the historically privileged student, i.e., enhanced social mobility and hegemonic reproduction of that privilege at the expense of the underprivileged.

In the classroom, instructors may use educational technology as a tool to introduce serious content and promote analytical thinking and problem-solving. Thus, access to a digital education is becoming increasingly difficult—unless one is a member of the historically privileged "class" who:

a) can afford domestic computer purchases and internet access;
b) possesses the requisite tax base to subsidise and implement quality educational technologies in her or his children's classrooms; and
c) because of (a) and (b), possesses the necessary computer literacy skills to enter and participate successfully in the twenty-first century's post-industrial, information age.

3.1. Technology-related Planning and Policies

Policies are guidelines for activity, put into writing and officially decreed or accepted by the organisation. In a sense, technology plans represent end points for which technology policies are a beginning and a road map. The goal of technology policies and plans is the successful integration of technology to support student learning and school management. In content terms, technology planning and policies address three major areas: vision, access, and integration. Vision pertains to what is expected from the technology overall. Access refers to the acquisition, deployment, and availability of technology to the target audiences. Integration of technology is the development and implementation of strategies that make technology useful and capable of accomplishing the vision.

Policies represent relative end states that begin with the adoption of a technology plan. This in turn involves a series of steps, ranging from the determination of needs, the involvement of stakeholders, and the ratification of a document, to the implementation, evaluation, and revision of the plan. Assessing plans and policies involves evaluating the content of plans and documenting the existence of policies, as well as assessing the process of plan development and implementation.

A technology plan serves as a bridge between traditional established standards and classroom practice. It articulates, organises, and integrates the content and processes of education in a particular discipline with appropriate technologies. It facilitates multiple levels of policy and curriculum decisionmaking, especially in schools and educational organisations that allow for supportive resource allocations.

Planning is a continuous, organisational process that provides "a road map". A plan for technology can maximise the potential of technological innovations while helping to overcome the challenges of implementation. Ultimately, it should result in more efficient expenditures and improved student achievement.

Implemented technology policies can be a background against which a technology plan is carried out, or they can be one desired end goal of the implementation of a technology plan. Examples of such policies might be acceptable use policies (AUPs) or policies related to the privacy of student data records. A school may have broader policies in place that will influence a technology plan, such as business policies that could include requirements for impact analyses, financial contingencies, or security safeguards. Policies with local impact can be adopted at any level, from the school to the district or region, or to the state as a whole.

There are different types of technology-related policies:

i) acceptable-use (or appropriate-use) policies (AUPs);

ii) restrictions on access to student records;

iii) technology security policies;

iv) policies regarding acceptance of commercial advertising on school websites;

v) policies regarding acquisition, maintenance or disposal of school equipment or applications;

vi) policies regarding acceptance of donated equipment and software;

vii) policies regarding community or after-school access to school or district technology resources.

All technology plans should take into account long-range funding issues; focus on instructional and administrative enhancements and goals; identify an implementation phase; coordinate all aspects of technology integration, including professional development or staff training; and evaluate outcomes. The stages of a pre-planning phase include a current-status assessment of technology, including equipment, skills, and use. Additionally, a current and future needs assessment provides the plan with direction and credibility.

Major plan components can include:

a) review of technology status, needs assessment, and other pre-planning products

b) vision/goal statements

c) equity issues

d) instructional uses of technology

e) student technology standards

f) staff technology standards

g) integration into core curriculum

h) pilot programme and action research

i) management uses of technology

j) student information systems

k) infrastructure and support for infrastructure, including such facilities-related needs as air conditioning/cooling and asbestos abatement

k) review of current "state of the art" for options in design of infrastructure

l) capabilities of hardware and software, projections of "next generation" capabilities and features

m) acceptance and management of donated computing resources

n) long-range goals

o) inventory control issues, such as maintenance and replacement cycle

p) budget projections and funding sources for initial installation, hardware, and software

q) staff training programmes

r) benchmarking standards

s) quality control components

t) security planning

There are potential components of a technology plan that can overlap with a school or district's facilities plan, such as network installation costs, including electrical wiring, maintenance and expansion. Technology planners and administrators will most likely want to decide in the pre-planning phase where to deal with facilities issues and related budgeting.

3.1.1. Implementation

Creating a technology plan and getting it approved and funded are only the beginning. Implementation has its own timeline and benchmarks, including purchasing equipment and installing, training, and evaluating each new technology introduced. The technology plan should account for each of these components, as well as implementers or teams responsible.

Perhaps the most important aspect of the technology plan process is evaluating its results and impact. Provisions for revising the plan should be a part of its creation, in the form of a review cycle that includes timelines and reporting. Possible components of the review cycle are listed below. If records from the pre-planning phase have been kept, the evaluation phase will be able to provide greater insight into the plan's progress and impacts. Possible means to obtain measures used to determine progress include customer feedback, plan audits, focus groups, and surveys.

It is important to remember that technology or parts of the plan that are not implemented should not be considered failures. Implementing new technology can be a daunting undertaking and flexibility is needed for any change process. For this reason, evaluation in a variety of formats is critical in objectively determining what is working and what needs more attention. Review cycle components include accountability measures, such as identification of indicators during pre-planning to maintain records of progress; technical performance; student performance; community support; implementation benchmarks; budget analyses; utilisation records; evaluation components; and progress measures.

Technology implementation is a continuous process that adapts to the organisation's changing circumstances and includes ongoing evaluation. Effective evaluation will force planners to rethink and adapt objectives, priorities, and strategies as implementation proceeds. Continuous evaluation also facilitates making changes if aspects of the plan are not working. Evaluating the implementation of a technology plan can be conducted by various means. Simple observations, both negative and positive, that have been made by students and teachers using the technology are the most helpful. Interviews and informal meetings with both instructors and students can draw out the lessons that both groups have learned from using the technology.

3.2. Financial Analysis of Technology

There are two aspects to the financing of technology (or any entity, for that matter): expenditures and revenues. Revenues would be fairly straightforward to discuss, but are less germane to financial analyses for technology than expenditures. School financial systems are not particularly well configured to identify and present the costs associated with deploying, maintaining, and upgrading technology in schools. Categories used for budgeting in connection with technology planning overlap poorly with the major categories used in school accounting.

Local and state requirements affect financial reporting practices, arguably more than they do any other area of data collection. The data elements available for analysis, and the way they are treated to produce reports, can vary widely within the bounds of generally accepted accounting principles (GAAP). This applies with particular force to the following aspects of cost accounting: the general allocation of functions to programmes; the allocation of costs for equipment purchases and support services; the definition of indirect costs; and the definition of bases for the allocation of indirect costs. Cost assignment and depreciation schedules for equipment are particular issues.

For the purpose of defining data elements in the financial area, there are two sorts of financial transactions or activities: revenues and other sources of funds; and expenditures and other uses of funds. Both revenues and expenditures have a number of aspects or dimensions:

i) *Revenues*: fund; revenue source; project/reporting code.

ii) *Expenditures*: fund; programme; function; object; project/reporting code; level of instruction; operational unit (building); subject matter; job classification; special cost center.

iii) *Fund*: A fiscal and accounting entity with a self-balancing set of accounts recording cash and other financial resources. It also contains all related liabilities and residual equities or balances. Funds are established to carry on specific activities or attain certain objectives of a local education agency (LEA) according to special legislation, regulations, or other restrictions.

Maintenance and support expenditures may be difficult to precisely ascertain because teachers and even students may be doing maintenance on a volunteer basis, or as staff hired only to perform those duties. Loss of productivity is another aspect of maintenance and support that may or may not be able to be determined or even considered in expenses.

3.3. Equipment and Infrastructure

The terms equipment and infrastructure refer to computer hardware and associated communications equipment and cabling, as well as other technology-related equipment regularly used in schools. Indicators address the availability, capabilities, and connectivity of computer equipment and infrastructure.

Computer equipment refers to both computers and associated peripheral equipment, such as:

i) computers, including desktop and laptop machines, but extending to handheld computers, mainframe machines, and other specialised computing devices; and

ii) peripheral equipment that may be attached to computers, such as monitors, keyboards, disc drives, modems, printers, scanners, cameras, and speakers.

Other technology resources in the school setting are also included, such as:

i) network devices—routers, hubs, switches, access servers;

ii) communications support, such as fax-back and voice-mail resources in regular use by instructional and administrative staff;

iii) videoconferencing and other distance education tools, including satellite transmitters and receivers, cable-based receivers, and modem or codec-based video equipment;

iv) projection devices, from transparent and opaque projectors to video monitors; and

v) graphing calculators and other specialised computational aids.

The term infrastructure covers both devices and cabling. Devices supporting technology in schools include specialised equipment (such as switches, routers, modems, or codecs) that link computers or video hardware to networks. Infrastructure also refers to cabling, whether wire, fibre optic, or coaxial. In newer systems, links between computers are wireless, in which case infrastructure refers to receivers and transmitters. For schools to use technology, they must first have it and make it available for students, teachers, and administrative staff. Acquiring that technology, from computers to modems to two-way conferencing equipment, is only one step in facilitating student learning. Curriculum integration and professional development are also essential components in this process.

Technology administrators will want to determine what qualifies a piece of equipment to be counted or not. They must pay careful attention to whether technology resources are actually available to their intended users when needed.

Instructional settings can be more than classrooms. Instructional settings include regular classrooms and computer laboratories, but any setting in which instruction takes place could be considered within this category, such as "pull-out" rooms for remedial or special education, for instance. Media centres (what used to be called libraries) might be included, as well as specialised laboratories (chemistry labs, for instance) or rooms dedicated to distance education. It is even possible that some instruction may take place off-campus and therefore be included as a setting in this category, especially in the case of laptop loan or grant programmes.

The presence of multimedia computers is an important indicator of technology capability. Such computers allow the user to display images, video, and sound as well as text, and therefore create opportunities for learning from a variety of media resources, or from resources that use these capabilities simultaneously. More exciting is the prospect that students can create multimedia reports and presentations themselves. Depending on the subject matter and teachers' preferences, such capabilities can expand the repertory of student capacities and create useful skills and forms of expression for use later in life.

If computer labs are a prominent component of technology access in school, it may be important to collect additional information. Indicators for the amount of time in the school week that students spend in the computer lab, or for the percentage of classes that regularly use the computer lab, may provide more detail to round out the picture of access. Computer-based curriculum planning and instructional management are much more likely to take place if teachers have dedicated computers exclusively for their use, because teachers have access to the resources when and where they are needed. Similarly, it is important to know if teachers have access to portable ("laptop") computers, since their work will often be done at home after the school day.

School leaders and support staff need computers to use data management systems which in turn can have great impact on decision making, improving educational management and, ultimately, student care and performance. It makes no sense to provide technology to support instruction and not for support of school management functions.

Creating an integrated management system can benefit all users in a school or district; information can usefully flow both from the teachers and the classroom to administrators, and from school management to instructional staff. For example, computer-based attendance systems allow for immediate administrative action upon a teacher recording an absence (i.e., a follow-up telephone call to the home or parent that same morning). Likewise, aggregate information on absences, health condition, and test results for a given student may help a teacher make educational decisions.

Users might want to break down administrative and support staff into narrower categories, such as student support personnel (counselors, social service specialists, health personnel), administrative support staff (transportation coordinators, attendance officers, dietitian/cafeteria manager), or leaders (principal, assistant principal, etc.).

Connection to a school local-area-network (LAN) or, through such a network, to a district-wide wide-area-network (WAN) greatly expands what can be done with a computer. Access to shared resources such as printers or shared memory, or to electronic mail, or to specialised instruments or computing devices, can support collective work and increase the efficient use of resources. Access to the Internet opens up a whole world of riches, with attendant risks. A limiting consideration is the amount of bandwidth (the term refers to the amount of information that can traverse the network each second) available to each computer.

3.3.1. Access, and Availability

Knowing the percentage of classrooms with computers does not necessarily indicate how many students use them, for example. Although direct assessments of actual use by students would be the most desirable indicator of availability, such measurement may be difficult to obtain. Availability, means that students, teachers, or administrative staff have access to, or can use, the technology in question, whenever needed. Access to current technologies, software, and telecommunications networks has been listed as an essential condition for both teachers and students to make use of technology as a powerful learning tool by the International Society for Technology in Education's (ISTE).

3.4. Technology Applications

The term technology applications refers to software and systems, run on school equipment, that support important administrative and instructional functions. The following functions represent the major categories of technology applications for schools and districts:

a) *Administrative management software and systems*: Financial accounting; staff attendance and payroll; budgeting; operations and planning, including transportation and food systems; facilities management; inventory control; and decision support;

b) *Instructional support software and systems*: Instructional planning and management, including grading, testing, and individualised educational programme (IEP) management; instructional support, including student attendance; access to remote educational resources; and distance education.

c) *Communications support*: Electronic mail; local- and wide-area networks; access to the internet and remote educational and administrative sites; satellite uplinks and downlinks; and internet-based telephony ("voice over IP," or voIP); operating systems; and security systems, such as firewall technology, secure transmission systems, and antivirus software.

Percentage of instructional applications aligned with one or more learning standards: Number of applications with ratings of three or four divided by the total number of instructional applications and converted to a percentage. May be for alignment with standards for all subjects, or for a specific curriculum area or grade. Following are the different types of Instructional application types:

i) Instructional process support;

ii) learning support (practice drills; problem solving; data analysis; simulation/demonstration; research; distance learning);

iii) assessment.

Teacher-support instructional applications: Software or applications specifically designed to support teachers in instructional processes. Examples include attendance software; grading applications; testing systems; student work or portfolio systems; lesson planning software.

The basic tool skills that everyone involved in schools—from the principal to the teacher to the student—must have in order to be able to use technology range from simple keyboarding to computer programming. While some skills obviously vary in complexity and may not be needed until higher education, basic capabilities have become part of a new literacy. Knowing them is akin to learning how to read in an earlier age: the mark of an educated, competent person. Assessing the extent to which the school technology offerings teach these tool skills is very important and will no doubt become even more so as technology becomes more transparent in the classroom.

Examples of application types that support technology tool skill development in instructional settings: word processors; spreadsheets; database software; desktop publishing; process writing software; keyboarding training software; telecommunications; web browsers and search engines; web authoring; presentation development software; programming tools, including compilers and interpreters. As applications and devices in use in classrooms continue to evolve, and as technology becomes further integrated into education, what are considered "basic tool skills" can be expected to evolve.

There are a number of important communication functions that schools and districts carry out which technology can enable or improve. Communication between school staff and parents of students can be supported through class homework assignment web pages or telephone hotlines. E-mail can support direct parent communication with teachers or the principal. Communication with the larger community is enabled by school web pages or online school "report cards"; the latter often become part of real estate agencies' electronic brochures for the community.

Schools use computer-based networks to conduct significant business with their districts, other institutions, and with state authorities. Data are sent to state education agencies; requests for purchases go back and forth from schools to central districts. Staff attendance records are forwarded to district payroll systems. Transcripts are sent to other schools or districts when students move, or to colleges when students graduate.

Although most of the public and policy focus on computing in schools addresses instructional uses, large gains in efficiency and effectiveness in schools can be made by using computers and network systems in administrative applications. Although such applications are decidedly less glamorous and less likely to be visible or appear reasonable to anxious parents worried about their children's future, they can play a critical role in making food services, transportation or records management work better and in reducing the management burden on senior administrators so they can maintain their focus on students' education.

Administrative software is also essential to the gathering, processing, and transmission of critical education data. Applications at the district level can be integrated into decision support tools. Strategic partnerships between schools and private corporations have resulted in technology forums, initiatives, and criteria to assist superintendents in choosing models to follow.

Standards for educational technology applications are being developed, with the potential to be used for assessment of instructional software and applications. Technical coordinators and other evaluators will have to develop criteria to evaluate the effectiveness of products beyond "best-of-breed" determinations. The situation is more problematic for evaluation of administrative software and applications. Standards for such applications do not exist or at least represent an entirely different framework. Schools and districts need to evaluate administrative software in terms of functional effectiveness.

Although information about technology applications is typically analysed at the school or district level, the relevant unit for data element definitions is the software programme or application. Unit records for software form the basic elements for a comprehensive technology application database. A system based on unit records would meet day-to-day administrative needs and support overall assessment and planning.

Computer-based technologies are in the process of becoming critical to achieving schools' mission. Areas in which applications may be considered mission-critical at present include:

i) finance, including payroll, accounting, and budgeting;

ii) operations and planning, especially transportation management; and

iii) instructional management, including attendance and grading.

Other functions are equally important to schools, but carrying them out on computers is still not widespread enough to be considered "critical". These include instructional support; special education support (including both expanded accessibility for instructional resources and integrated education plan management); electronic mail; and communication with parents and community, especially via the web.

Administrative software packages used by most schools store student profiles, grades, attendance and discipline records. Testing companies can provide electronic versions of their scoring reports that include student-specific information. Additionally, scanners permit districts to automate tabulation of surveys and other local data collections. Availability and compatibility of data are no longer a barrier.

A greater challenge than collecting data is creating a process to transform the data into easily accessible, useful information that staff members will employ for school improvement.

3.5. Accessing Maintenance and Support Systems

In the early stages of implementation of technology in schools, the need for maintenance is often unanticipated. Volunteers are pressed into service, or teachers with an interest in technology are assigned support roles in addition to their other obligations. Such systems and roles are difficult to sustain. It is a hallmark of the institutionalisation of technology that more formal systems for maintenance and support have been established.

Current trends in support for technology systems include the establishment of more formal technology support structures, often using helpdesk software to track requests for support and responses; at the other extreme of the spectrum, trends include the incorporation of students in middle and secondary school as sources of technical help and outsourcing to non-school persons or entities, either on a volunteer or more formal contract basis. It is worth emphasising that in the latter situation, as with any situation in which work products depend on persons not under the control of the organisation, proper documentation is an essential requirement and should be made an explicit part of any outsourcing contract or agreement.

Much of the information that a school or district needs to assess the status of maintenance and support systems can be extracted from a database on inventory and maintenance of hardware and software. Indicators are provided below for measuring both maintenance and support of technology resources in school administrative and instructional settings and for assessing the roles of personnel providing that support to teachers, students, and administrative staff.

Maintenance means those preventive, diagnostic, updating, replacement, and repair procedures that a school or district has in place. Maintenance can be provided either by persons who are part of the school system or through an outsourced contract. It includes documenting trends and patterns in the use of applications or equipment. Specific maintenance items might include:

i) periodic replacement of parts and renewal of consumable supplies;

ii) repair or replacement of faulty components;

iii) periodic inspection and cleaning of equipment;

iv) updating or upgrading hardware and software, including installing new operating system versions;

v) adding or deleting users from a system, or modifying user rights and properties;

vi) periodic backup of stored files on a school network;

vii) monitoring the condition and functionality of networks and equipment, including testing website accesses and links; and

viii) installing and removing equipment and applications.

The term support refers to actions taken on behalf of users rather than to actions taken on equipment and systems. Support denotes activities that keep users working or help users improve the ways they work. Included under support might be such items as:

a) help desks and other forms of putting a person in touch with another person to resolve a problem or provide advice;

b) automated information systems, such as searchable frequently-asked-question (FAQ) databases or newsletters;

c) initial training and familiarisation tours for equipment and software, whether automated or conducted by a human;

d) instructional and curriculum integration support, usually through observation and personal interaction between a teacher and a technology coordinator; and

e) technology integration support for administrative applications, usually conducted through specialised consultants or software/systems vendors.

f) As with maintenance, support can be delivered through a variety of mechanisms, including in-house technology specialists, external volunteers, or outsourced contracts.

Technology has not yet fully established itself in the school setting, as it has in many business sectors. When the network goes down in a school or district, the administrators, teachers, and students just wait until it comes back up. Any information lost may not be restored. In the instructional setting, preparing for an outage may mean that teachers file printouts as backup materials. The same outage in the business world can cost hundreds of thousands of dollars in lost sales; lost instructional time has not been valued in the same way. Yet, as schools rely more and more on the use of technology (both administratively and instructionally), the loss of time and information is increasingly understood to be expensive and disruptive to the learning process.

Maintenance and backup systems are therefore begining to be recognised as important throughout the school setting.

As schools commit more funds to the purchase of technology, they must also look at the support needed by the end users of these purchases. Most school systems have designated an office of technology support, but rarely do tech support personnel work directly with school staff. Usually, the only times tech support visits a school is when there is a major infrastructure malfunction or new equipment is being installed. Even more rarely can central-office technology support personnel be of assistance in educating users, say, on how a software package works.

The majority of support personnel time is focused on acquiring, installing, and maintaining hardware and the technology infrastructure. The ratio of end users (or computers) to professional support personnel is generally very high. As schools record the levels of support staffing and maintenance incidents, they can work to determine acceptable support ratios. Much support for instructional staff comes from volunteer or part-time technology coordinators, working on donated time or in addition to other instructional obligations. Help desks are still a relative rarity. Use of students in these roles is not uncommon.

3.6. Technology-related Professional Development

Teachers and students would use technological tools-or-not-in learning situations, depending on whether they helped one to learn in that context. If research were required, students would conduct it at the school digital library or at a remote resource as needed. School administrative records and cafeteria food requirements would be updated automatically from entry-screening systems, or perhaps the attendance software on a teacher's personal digital assistant (PDA). But the technological tools available do not fit together this seamlessly yet, and teachers and staff (and students) need training and professional development in order to make the best use of technology in schools. In fact, providing sufficient development and training to give staff skills and confidence in the use of technology is widely viewed as an ongoing challenge to schools.

The term professional development to represent learning activities of all kinds for school staff that prepare them to use technology in the school setting. Included under the term are activities such as the following:

i) familiarisation with the operation of equipment and software;
ii) development of proficiency in the use of the technology "tools" to carry out school tasks;
iii) the application of software and applications to the management of school activities, whether instructional or administrative; and
iv) the integration of technology into teaching, learning, and administrative processes.

Professional development is explicitly understood to extend to administrative and support staff whose jobs have changed and will continue to change due to the infusion of technology in schools. Professional development includes support for teachers and staff as they apply technology to their evolving practices, from lesson plans and curriculum integration to record keeping and administrative functions. It is an ongoing process that cannot be satisfied with one-time training in a particular technology.

The methods and content of technology-related professional development are changing as quickly as technology itself. Technology has brought a windfall for delivery methods in professional development. Online delivery means can help educators to find the best time for training based on their own schedules. Video and audio conferencing allow teachers access to both instructional and collegial support. E-mail and e-bulletin boards enable teachers to share information and solve problems. Still, taken as a whole, technology cannot solve the problem of allocating the time needed for ongoing professional development to establish and maintain proficiency in technology use. There are many competing demands for teachers' and administrators' time, and districts need to allocate sufficient time and resources for professional development and training.

Tailoring evaluation methods to professional development programmes makes sense—data on how teachers and administrators progress and how they are using new technologies to promote student achievement give great insight into what technology is doing for schools. By evaluating professional development, technology planners and administrators can learn what is working, and what or who needs help.

The relevant unit for professional development data element definitions is the single training event or programme. Single training event unit records form the basic elements for a comprehensive professional development database. A system based on training event unit records would meet day-to-day administrative needs and support overall assessment and planning. For each training/professional development event attended by at least one staff member at the school or district level, the following data elements are recorded:

i) Event starting date

ii) Event ending date

iii) Event name

iv) Total duration (seat time), hours

v) Event type

vi) Mode of delivery

vii) Benchmarks, standards, or mandated curriculum areas (specified by state or district) covered in the course

viii) Contribution (number of hours) to minimum district or state-specified requirement

ix) Number of hours per academic year required by district or state

x) Roster of participating staff (with individual identifiers if available; job classification)

3.6.1. Standards of Professional Development

Quality professional development, structured and provided

within a context of ongoing school improvement planning and a culture of collaboration, improves and sustains the capacity of the adult learner to:

a) *Standard 1*: use inquiry and reflective practice within the learning community. Educators keep journals to record and reflect on their own practice; time is allocated at school improvement and staff meetings to share journal content and to review curriculum, instruction, and assessment techniques, and process exists to make appropriate changes.

b) *Standard 2*: learn from recognised resources within both the public and private sectors, from successful models, and from colleagues and others in the learning community.

c) *Standard 3*: identify personal and adult learning needs and styles, and select appropriate modes of participation. Educators have the opportunity to complete learning style inventories and to select professional development compatible with individual learning styles.

d) *Standard 4*: implement research-based leadership strategies to support and sustain ongoing developmental activities.

e) *Standard 5*: integrate technologies as tools to assist with the curriculum development, instructional management, and assessment practices.

f) *Standard 6*: invest time in an ongoing process of collegial dialogue, collaborative learning, and exploration of new and/or proven instructional strategies.

3.7. E-Rate: Equalising Access to Technologies

Computers and the internet have become widely available in today's public schools, and most parents would be surprised not to see a computer in their child's classroom. In particular, once glaring differences in the availability of computers and the internet between high- and low-poverty schools have all but disappeared. And, although classroom-level internet access is still more common in wealthy schools, there have been increases in classroom access in the poorest schools since 1998, after a period of relative stagnation.

The importance of education in a free society-and, more broadly, open access to information-is undiminished today. Poor and minority children are less likely to have access to computers and the Internet at home. Schools help reduce this inequity in access to technology. Nearly 90 per cent of Americans support the introduction of educational technology into American schools and libraries, and most (83 per cent) see the internet as a way to improve educational opportunities for all Americans, especially for disadvantaged children. According to many proponents, increasing the educational uses of computers and the internet may provide an opportunity to transform teaching, predicting a move toward more student-centered instruction based on content-rich real-world applications—what some have called the transformation of the classroom teacher from "the sage on the stage" to "the guide on the side".

The E-Rate has its roots in the 1930s when, concerned about unequal access to telephones, US Congress initiated a programme of publicly supported "universal service" to ensure that poor and geographically isolated communities would not be excluded from the first American "information revolution". The 1934 Communications Act sought to "make available, so far as possible, to all the people of the United States, a rapid, efficient nationwide, and worldwide wire and radio communication service with adequate facilities at reasonable charges."

E-Rate is intended to provide financial assistance to schools and libraries for the purpose of equalising access among poor and geographically isolated communities to telecommunications and advanced digital technologies. Isolated rural schools also benefited, with higher E-Rate discounts going to rural schools at which up to half of the students receive subsidised school meals. Other evidence shows that schools have actively sought to expand the availability of digital technology: Virtually every public school is now connected to the Internet; connections exist in nearly eight out of 10 public school classrooms; and faster dedicated lines are quickly replacing slower dial-up service access to the internet.

At a minimum, then, it appears that the E-Rate has provided a partial "financial bridge" across the digital divide separating the poor, minorities, and geographically isolated from equitable access to computers and the internet. As part of the application process, schools and libraries are required to provide information on both their existing level of services and that planned after the receipt of ERate discounts.

This includes data on the number of phones per student (not per teacher), the number of internet-connected computers per student, the number of teleconferencing links per student, the fraction of buildings connected to the internet, the fraction of classrooms connected to the internet, the total number of internet connections per student, and the highest speed of these internet connections (phone, direct, and overall).

About two-thirds of students in public E-Rate schools have teachers who reportedly have access to their school's computer network from home, and over half of these students have teachers who can also access the internet from home through their school's network. Such home access is important, as it provides greater opportunities for teachers to use the internet both for professional development and to plan classroom instruction, and also provides the opportunity to use digital technology for purposes such as recordkeeping and communication with students, peers, and parents.

Students in the poorer E-Rate schools are less likely to have teachers who report such home access than students in wealthier E-Rate schools, controlling for differences in school size, location, and grade level. Students in rural E-Rate schools are estimated to be 14 percentage points less likely to have teachers who can access the internet from home through their school's computer network than students in suburban E-Rate schools, controlling for the same school characteristics.

Most students in E-Rate schools also have teachers who reportedly have access to an e-mail account at their school, but there are statistically significant differences by school characteristics.

References

Barker, Roz, "The Internet and information skills—a primary school perspective", *Scan*, 15(1), February, pp.14-15, 1996.

Barkhouse, Nancy, "Grasping the thread: Web page development in the elementary classroom", *Emergency Librarian*, 24(3), January-February, pp.24-25, 1997.

Boling, Elizabeth and Kirkley, Sonny, "Helping students design World Wide Web documents", *TIE (Telecommunications in Education) News*, 8(4), August, pp.16-22, 1997.

Bourke, Jane, Using the Internet to Research, *Ready-Ed Publications*, Perth, Western Australia, 1997.

Burgstahler, Sheryl, *New Kids on the Net: A Network Sampler: Internet Activities for K-12*, Allyn and Bacon, New York, 1997.

Butterworth, Margaret, ed., *Information Technology in Schools: Implications for Teacher Librarians*, 3rd edn, Australian Library and Information Association, School Libraries Section (WA Group), Perth, 1997.

Glasscock, Alison, "The Internet and information skills—a secondary perspective", *Scan*, 15(1), February, pp.16-17, 1996.

Johnson, Doug, "Student access to Internet: librarians and teachers working together to teach higher level survival skills", *Emergency Librarian,* 22(3), January-February, pp.8-12, 1995.

McCullen, Caroline, "World Wide Web in the classroom: the quintessential collaboration", *Learning and Leading With Technology*, 23(3), November, pp.7-10, 1995.

4

Restructuring the School Curriculum

Computers are no longer placed in isolated rooms with locked doors to be opened only by an ICT teacher. Instead, subject-area teachers, administrators, and librarians all use them and other ICT equipment whenever these are needed in their working places. Ideally, the same is true for students. In and out of lessons, they use computers when needed: in classrooms, auditoria and labs, in the library, in rooms available for project activities and homework preparation. Sometimes students use smart keyboards for taking notes at a lecture, or palm computers when going out of school to conduct environmental projects. At other times, students use digital cameras. Computerised equipment is also used to monitor students' health. The entire school is immersed in the information space. Computers in teachers' and students' homes (school laptops and notebooks, shared by teachers, is one option) play an important role in the learning environment.

When administrators and decisionmakers think about using computers in schools, the most obvious obstacle is cost of hardware. The nub of the problem is that few school buildings would be able to contain enough desktop computers for every student in every lesson. Most schools in both developed and developing countries are over 50 years old. Some have existed for over a century. Classroom spaces were designed to reflect the traditional instructional style with little, if any, thought given to investigation-based, group learning, let alone fibre-optic cabling.

While some funding is available for renovation and rebuilding, the short-term reality for most schools is that existing spaces must be adapted to accommodate new learning technologies. New or (re-)designed schools, and old schools, are thinking how to create more flexible space for ICT use. Traditional technologies like pen, paper, and blackboard will continue along with the newer ICT, which means leaving enough space on each student's desk for writing as well for a monitor.

4.1. Arrangements of ICT in Classrooms

Here is a list of options for space arrangements of people and ICT in a typical classroom:

a) The whole class listening to one person presenting from the front, possibly through telecommunication.
b) Equipment needed is a computer with a screen visible by the speaker, together with a projector and screen. To demonstrate an object, conduct an experiment, or show videotapes additional equipment is needed. To speak in a big auditorium a microphone is also needed.
c) Whole class discussion of a theme with questions asked and answered.
d) Equipment needed is the same as above, with a computer screen available for someone to take notes. To record the discussion, you need audio-video recording devices.
e) Individual work by all students in a classroom (essay writing, testing, studying new software).
f) Dividing the class into halves, with one each group doing individual work in an audio-visual environment.
g) Moving between zones
h) Individual work outside classroom (homework, distant tutoring).

4.1.1. Desktop Computers

Today, the desktop computer is the major ICT device in schools as well as generally in the world outside schools. School principals, ICT-coordinators, and teachers have to confront the problem of space design for desktops. The space design of the computer-equipped classroom reflects three different models:

i) A teacher's computer with a projector (used by students also).

ii) Several computers for group work in parallel with other activities (in primary school, language and science labs).

iii) A dedicated computer lab that provides ICT access to all students, or, if this is not possible, to half a class at a time.

4.1.2. Visual Channel of Information

In the traditional school, this channel was important for both the student and teacher. To the student, it allows:

i) seeing teachers and images as they talk; and

ii) seeing a text in a textbook or workbook.

To the teacher, it allows:

i) seeing the process of writing or conducting experiments by students, receiving non-verbal reaction from students; and

ii) preventing students from seeing what other students are doing in exams.

Teachers can see on their screen all student screens, or the individual screen of any student. The teacher should control lighting and especially sunlight entering the room. Special window coverings and electrical lights section to be turned off during large screen presentation should be planned. During projection, the room light should be bright enough (40-50 foot candles) for student interaction, not just dim for note taking, but no more than 3-5 foot candles of ambient room light should fall on the screen. This can be done by creating lighting zones in the classroom, setting apart the student seating area, the front presentation area, and the lectern/projector area. Computer noise should be as low as possible; others should not hear the sound emanating from any student's computer.

Desk space is designed and limited to a single student with a (paper) notebook and sometimes a book. There is frequently not enough space left for a desktop computer. The CPU can be placed under the table. This creates some inconveniences: for example, most of the computers' diskette and CD-ROM slots, power button, and interface sockets are located on the front panel of the CPU box, but some sockets are on the reverse side and it is hard (but amusing for students, of course) to manipulate all of these underneath the desk.

The keyboard should always be at hand, and it needs plenty of space. Nevertheless, the normal position for a keyboard is below the normal height of a desk. An optional flat drawer unrolling from the bottom side of the desk is therefore preferable. It is important that communication and power lines do not interfere with physical movements in a classroom or auditorium. For example, a portable projector is a good idea, but you should be very careful where you place cables so that students do not stumble over them during lessons.

In many cases, wiring becomes a major problem in ICT installation, taking up a good proportion of the costs. Although not absolutely necessary, raised flooring allows for easier reconfiguration of classrooms. Traditional classroom layouts work especially well when the computer is integrated into the desk because wires and cables can be completely hidden, allowing narrower aisles while facilitating access to network interface and electric outlets. An interesting new design idea is to make the school desk triangular, which also helps solve the problem of changing the student's object of vision from the computer to the teacher and back.

Desks in classrooms can be movable, to be reconfigured for different functions in the room. For example, individual triangular desks can be reorganised into hexagonal tables for group work. Different layouts are used in classrooms oriented to the extensive use of computers:

i) Rows
ii) "L" configurations
iii) "U" configurations

iv) Clusters of four desks

v) Clusters of six desks

4.1.2.1. Computer chairs

Computer chairs that allow students to assume proper ergonomic postures should be selected. Students who spend many hours at a computer both at home and in the classroom run the same risks of cumulative trauma disorders as office workers, yet they have less control of the environments in which they work. Standard classroom chairs that do not meet these needs put students at risk.

Chairs need to possess the following attributes:

i) *height adjustability (preferably pneumatic).* Ease of adjustment insures that students can achieve proper posture.

ii) *back tilt.* The facility to tilt a chair back is a useful feature that enables students to adjust eye-to-monitor distance within the space allowed.

iii) *durability and tip resistance.* Look for solid welds and heavy-duty mechanisms. A good test of tip resistance is to raise the chair to its highest position and hang a heavy jacket or book bag on the chair back.

iv) *a broad seat and back design with adequate comfort with minimal sculpting.* This design meets the needs of a large percentage of users. Although lumbar support and forward-tilt functions may be necessary in an office, it is more important to make users comfortable. Students usually present a greater range of body sizes than the office worker population.

There are alternatives to the familiar desktop computer, and followingh are some of these.

4.1.2.2. Portable computers (notebooks)

Some schools can afford to give students their own computer, one that is lightweight, small, and inexpensive, shock-, drop, and water-proof and connected to a network in and outside school. Notebooks today:

i) have full-functional operating systems;

ii) are more expensive than desktops;

iii) weigh about 3 kilograms, and can be damaged when dropped on a concrete floor; and are portable—you can use them in any lesson you need, not in the place where a computer is constantly mounted.

iv) Schools should take the option of notebooks seriously. It is true that prices are nearly twice as high as for desktops. However, this is less serious a limitation in view of the costs of other hardware, networking, software, maintenance, and training.

Apart from cost, there are other discouraging factors for using notebooks that include:

i) physical damage (by dropping or pouring liquid);

ii) thievery (of an easy movable and valuable object); and

iii) lack of personal responsibility (in the case of school ownership).

One solution could be to store computers on a cart or trolley that can be locked up at the end of the day. A notebook computer, printer, and LCD-projector on a trolley in a radio-network environment constitute a valuable combination in the case of limited resources. Of course, the level of interactivity and hands-on experience in this model is limited if you have only one trolley for a whole school.

4.1.2.3. Individual computers

Affordable alternatives to notebooks, are the following:

i) smart keyboard;

ii) palm computers; and

iii) sub-notebooks.

A smart keyboard delivers the major text applications (text-editing spreadsheets, and email) and has a corresponding input device. They are functional in a school network or in association with a real computer. To reduce costs, internal memory, interfaces, and batteries are minimal. The result is still not cheap, because the product is not yet mass-produced. However, should a government decide to issue these to all schools in a country, prices are sure to fall substantially, to perhaps 10-20 per cent of a notebook.

Palm computers and sub-notebooks can provide interesting alternatives as well. Even today, these devices can provide certain critical applications like Internet connectivity for a small fraction of the cost of desktops. At the same time, these and other thin client computers can all be made robust and unbreakable, they can be individualised, and they are less attractive to thieves.

There are two further affordable choices. The first was based on that early ICT classic—the calculator. Extended to being almost a computer, this tool is useful for mathematics, physics and ICT classes. A second emerging option is an ultra-portable projector about the size and weight of a camera that can be connected to a computer instead of its monitor. The price of these today is more than for a computer, but that is expected to come down. Finally, in the near future we might expect wearable computers in schools. The computer here consists of a VR-helmet—output device and gloves—and a handheld input device. The computer is connected to the internet, to other school computers, and to peripherals via a wireless network, or sometimes cables. Students will have these computers with them continually and use them in all lessons.

4.1.3. Distributed Learning Network

The school can be organised in such a way that the school's central information network is available in every room, which means an output device (monitor) and an input device (keyboard and mouse) with corresponding interfaces. There are also the options of stylus, finger (at touch screens), and joystick for internet surfing. In schools of the near future, we can imagine individual keyboards and helmets for all students, and many screens, mostly projection and flat-panel. The large projection screens in an auditorium will be used primarily with teacher or student presentations.

Touch screens will be used for special occasions of choosing from a menu. The price for wired networking an entire school can be very high though costs can be reduced if some of the installation is done during school construction. Wireless networks, infrared or radiofrequency in classrooms and in buildings, are less expensive than cable networks, and their reliability and information transfer rates are improving rapidly.

The presence of networked computers for out-of-class access in different places such as corridors, for instance, can be exploited productively in some schools, but may become tempting to vandals in other cases. As ICT become more pervasive, computer-based equipment will be integrated into every aspect of a school's operation.

4.1.3.1. Role of library

In most schools, the library has for centuries been a place of less restricted, more individual, and more open work than a classroom. It has been the heart of our modern information civilisation. In the last few decades, school libraries have begun to accommodate, not only books, magazines, newspapers, art creations, but also transparent media for projection, audio-cassettes, 16mm movies, then videos and CDs, and now, DVDs.

The natural expansion of the library's function is to provide ICT technology as well, including resources like high-speed Internet connection, satellite TV, collection of CDs and DVDs, plus a limited amount of paper for printing, and removable computer storage such as discs and flash cards. However, there are problems connected with this most promising location. The first is space and number of available computer workstations. When librarians post up sign-up sheets, the usual finding is that:

i) everyone shows up,

ii) if not, the reservation is cancelled and someone else comes instead,

iii) the timetable is fully booked weeks ahead, even with limits imposed of, say, an hour a day with a maximum of three hours a week.

4.1.4. Use of Computers in Lecturing

Teachers are going to use multimedia projectors in lectures, which means they will also need:

i) a computer as the source of video and audio signals;

b) an extension cord to plug into the power line (assuming there is a socket in the class);

c) a screen to project on (projecting on a wall can be poor quality; on a whiteboard, it can be even worse);

c) a table to place a projector on;

d) curtains on windows because sunlight interferes with projected images; and

e) cables.

4.1.5. Computer Use in Primary Classes

The model of a kindergarten or primary school classroom where children are involved in different, sometimes even unrelated, activities looks like gaining over the traditional school where all children sit in rows and are usually engaged on the same task. Computers in quantities of one to ten can considerably enrich this multi-centre, multiple activities model. One of the possibilities here is to have a computer as a part, sometimes the centre of activity of a group of three-seven students. Activities of different groups can be different or the same.

4.1.5.1. Language lab

Another useful ICT installation in schools is the language lab. This has many of the features of the language lab that was popular before the computer era. The minimal model uses an audio source—a loudspeaker powered by a compact disk or magnetic tape player. A common problem is a different level of loudness for students who sit in different places in the classroom or who have other hearing problems. Individual headphones can solve this. The next step is to distribute the audio signal over an electronic network of students' headphones. We have now an opportunity for individualising instruction but it brings an immediate problem of communication with the teacher.

The more sophisticated language lab gives individual audio and, then, video feeds to all students. Microphones are provided for students' feedback and recording, which can be monitored and checked by the teacher and individual learners (and, in an ICT environment by a computer speech-recognition system). To avoid disturbing others, students are placed into partly transparent, partly sound-absorbing carrels. In the language context, the computer can:

i) integrate all types of information and communication;
ii) immerse students into virtual reality of another country and language;
iii) recognise human speech in some languages;
iv) supervise the learning process to a certain extent; and
v) visualise and audio-ise for teachers the stage of progress of all students.

The computerised classroom provides effective support for written and oral communication, and so it is desirable to have enough ICT for any language arts lesson. The typical problem here is the small number of computers per classroom. In fact, this is perhaps the major reason to look for portable computers with limited power.

4.1.5.2. Science lab

Specific applications of ICT in science learning are based on data collection and analyses done with sensors. A science lab can have, for example, six computers as part of a workshop for teamwork or individual data loading. Palm computers (and, to some extent, data loggers) are more effective and provide greater flexibility with sensor applications in science investigations than do desktop computers. At the same time, at least one desktop computer is needed to run virtual experiments in virtual labs using other instruments.

4.1.6. Teachers' Room

ICT in the teachers' room is an efficient way to support the information culture in schools and to invite more teachers to participate. A teacher's workstation—a computerised system with a word processor, graphics editor, scanner, camera, modem, and printer—allows teachers to save time and to increase productivity in such activities as:

i) preparing and updating daily lesson
ii) plans, making hard copy visualisations
iii) and handouts for classes, as well
iv) as individualised educational plans
v) for slower students and students with
vi) disabilities or with special problems;
vii) presenting visual/aural content materials,
viii) tasks, and questions to the audience;
ix) maintaining grade books;
x) compiling a data bank of exam questions;
xi) online inspection and correction of students' work on their computers; and
xii) keeping records, chronicles, and archives of all the above-mentioned events and proceedings with fast retrieval and easy access to any entry.

4.1.6.1. Computer Lab

In most of the school computer labs of the twentieth century, students learned how to use computers but were rarely asked to apply their skills outside the lab. In the twenty-first century, the situation will be different. The computer lab today is the space where:

i) specific technologies are learned by students and teachers when needed in short modules;
ii) lessons in different subjects (testing, essay writing) can be given; and
iii) after-school projects and individual work with the use of whole variety of ICT are happening.

The advantages of using a lab are ease of planning and technical support. There is more responsibility, and so it is easier to achieve safety and maintenance requirements. In the computer-saturated school, there could still be reasons to keep the computer lab as the place of qualified support and the source of all types of ICT hardware and software for school needs. Since there are rarely enough computers for all students in a class, a possible solution is for some students to work on computers while others work on non-computer activities related to the same project.

4.1.7. Virtual Classrooms

In the future, more learning will occur outside school buildings. Creating virtual classrooms where students can log in and find course notes, resources, worksheets and teaching tips, enables students who are home bound, out of school for sport or cultural activities, or on fieldtrips, to maintain contact with their coursework and teachers. This applies to non-traditional students as well as to older students, retirees, or those undergoing professional continuing education. Many schools are pursuing this method of creating a virtual school, that is, an online community of students, staff and parents with internet access at home or work.

This networked community tears down classroom walls and enables teachers to utilise home computers to extend the school's capabilities. Online communications are enabled and students can work on projects from school or home. Students who are ill, or absent for other reasons, can maintain contact. This kind of networking also helps individualised learning. Virtual classrooms and virtual schools can be shared by different real world schools and supported from the outside. Today, you can find many virtual classrooms on the Internet. This concept of the virtual classroom leads us to the modern ICT interpretation of the idea and the term open learning.

4.1.7.1. School information space

There are other different places where ICT may be found in

schools like the school principal's office and the custodian's room. All these should be integrated: learning spaces of students, teaching spaces of teachers, and administrative space of school administration, are parts of a common school information space technically accessible to all participants of the educational process. The principal, looking for the administrative record of a student can move to her recent project work and send a message to her teacher.

4.1.7.2. Orphanages and other special schools

Orphanages, correctional schools, reformatories, and other types of educational institutions where children have limited access to the world beyond their walls are places where ICT can make a radical difference. ICT can provide a channel for free information flow, distance education, contact with peers from other, similar organisations and families, as well as with psychological help and support. The same is true in a different sense for schools that might be special in different ways. For example, in schools for gifted children, contact with similar schools from other countries, as well as direct communication with the corresponding creative community provided by ICT, are important.

4.1.8. Implementing New Goals

In view of the swift progress in microelectronic technologies, it is remarkable that the basic computer environment has remained as stable as it has. The first Macintosh computer that introduced the multi-Windows desktop and major applications about a quarter of a century ago had only 128K of memory and did not have a hard disc. Yet the screen metaphor of the desktop in which the user works now is the same as it was then. What this means for schools is this: those with less powerful ICT or even none at all, can nevertheless develop new learning models that conform to the potential of ICT.

In other words, schools can begin to teach a mastery of the new literacy before the full panoply of equipment arrives. The technology used can be quite simple—a camera with black and white film, a radio, a newspaper, an encyclopedia, pen and paper. For some countries it sounds historical, but for others this provides a practical way to a knowledge society through education. Sometimes, a chance to assemble or fix a transparent low-tech device can give more understanding of high-tech than applying an opaque high-tech device.

The very experience of making oneself known to other people and getting the same message from them in return is a palpable metaphor for the world wide web. The impact of such an experience can be more meaningful than the short-time Internet connections of the uninitiated. The real success can be achieved in education not only by affluent societies where a computer in every family is the norm, but also by those developing countries that respect and cherish their human potential and creative heritage.

4.1.9. ICTs in Curriculum Development

At every level of schooling, ICT are not a closed or self-contained subject to be taught and learned independently from other subjects. Rather, ICT are a subject that, by its very nature, should be treated as interdisciplinary, integrative, and cross-curricular. The project-oriented method of teaching and learning, introduced through the use of ICT, will help both teachers and students become more conscious of their own capacities and responsibilities. Of course, some elements of ICT can be taught in a dedicated time.

However, it is important to support learning by an immediate application of technology that is meaningful and relevant to students. In any case, introductory lessons in any specific aspect of ICT (constituting a module of learning) should not continue for more than a few hours (and, better, for just a lesson). However, even here, the task must make concrete sense for students right from the start. The major module of intensive technical training is touch-typing, a skill for communicating between human beings and computers and which, naturally, needs fluency.

Microworld-like environments allow children from the age of 3 upwards to learn and use ICT for usual applications (graphics and text editing), and for modelling the real world and multimedia implementation of virtual realities. The introduction to a microworld or any specific feature or application of it should not take more than few minutes before the first action of a child to achieve something.

In planning their class schedules, different teachers should think about the information resources of the school and their access to them during their lessons. If the physical space of a school is seriously limited, the task of planning for ICT access is even more difficult. Long-distance learning has its own special time structuring. Different options for synchronous and asynchronous learning are possible and supported by ICT.

A common indicator of ICT development in schools is number of students per computer. However, another quantitative factor is even more relevant: the number of hours a week that computers are available for use. Of course, it is harder to optimise this parameter, than it is to put in a request for more hardware. Nevertheless, any school can set as a goal to make ICT available to students and teachers 12 hours a day, seven days a week. The implementation of this goal can also generate income for schools because this schedule would also allow the general public to come to school for ICT services when they are not being used by students and teachers.

4.2. Barriers of ICTs in Schools

In the early years of the twenty-first century, personal computers, accompanied by peripheral devices, have been virtually declared obligatory for educational institutions in all economically developed (and many developing) countries. There is substantial evidence supporting the idea that the new information and communication technologies (that is, ICT) are already capable of bringing about spectacular positive change to the whole fabric of general education. The prospects for the foreseeable future are truly overwhelming.

Schools and teachers face unprecedented pressure to get technology, get networked, and go online. At times, during this headlong rush to introduce new technologies, it is possible to forget what it is all for. To be sure, computers can raise student achievement in mathematics, languages, and other disciplines, but they have to be placed in the right hands and used in the right ways. Teachers and student roles might look like in an ICT-infused school. There are three main obstacles to the spread of these promising innovations:

i) the cost of ICT hardware, software and maintenance, although falling over the years, is still unaffordable to a majority of schools in many countries;

ii) the (often unconscious) resistance of many educators to the intrusion of still obscure technological newcomers that threaten to alter drastically long-established and time-honoured practices and customs; and

iii) the lack of teachers who are trained to exploit ICT proficiently.

Technology-rich curricula materials are therefore rarely implemented because students and teachers often have insufficient access to technology, and schools are unable to rearrange the curriculum to exploit the advantages of these materials. ICT hardware and software were initially designed and developed for non-educational purposes, and are thus poorly fitted physically for ordinary classrooms, especially in elementary schools. Available computers often do not work, which is aggravated by lack of maintenance support and inadequate software. This low and unreliable access to technology means that students do not get enough experience to master complex software tools, and teachers cannot assign tasks that assume ready computer availability.

The rigid structure of the classical system of schooling. Rooted in the educational paradigm of the eighteenth and nineteenth centuries, this kind of school could gain little from modern ICT unless it is radically transformed in its constitutive principles. In fact, most educators are not ICT-resistant, but the system in which they work under undoubtedly is. Technology (information or any other) brings little benefit unless it is skilfully and thoughtfully conducted and managed by teachers to enhance students' capacity to learn. Never before has the mission of school teachers been so heavily loaded as today. With the need for more independence, creativity, as well as the ability to engage in teamwork, the role of the individual in society is becoming more and more important. Today, it is natural to wish to design a school that is oriented towards developing these attributes, which can be done for all age groups, based on ICT.

One of the natural features of learning by doing that is facilitated by ICT is the similarity between the educational activity of a student and the activity of an adult at work. Student-journalists and student-researchers, for example, can produce significant results, even if they are only eight years old. Similarly, middle school students (12 to 16 years old) can provide technical service, expertise and consulting in regard to ICT.

Students can participate in choosing equipment and software, its installation, repair, and even the technical training of teachers. They can also participate in lessons as technical support experts. Teamwork and working with younger children provide many possibilities. By using the computer as an environment, a tool, and an agent, to design, create, and explore model worlds, students get unprecedented opportunities to see, analyse, and reflect on every step of their own learning processes, thus acquiring mastery, not only of the subject matter, but also in the art of learning.

The social climate in many academic settings is often fraught with competition and isolation. Where collaborative and cooperative learning opportunities are increased, achievement scores are known to rise, and students respect the contribution that each person offers, regardless of differences in ability, background, or handicap. Instead of fearing differences in one another, they look for ways to tap the unique and individual areas of strength for the benefit of all. A collaborative approach paves the way for a radical re-shaping of the content and procedures of the general school curriculum. Practical implementation of these kinds of transformation become possible when supported by advanced ICT to create powerful learning environments.

Teachers can carry the important mission of being agents of change, not only in ICT, but also in the whole system of education since ICT are the instruments that can launch an important and general paradigm shift. In this case, one teacher might naturally blend several technologies as a productive starting point for the integration of ICT into all learning activities. In fact, it is often the case that teachers of material technology, who start simply with an idea of applying technologies for human needs, make better, more creative use of ICT than teachers who start with the conception of the value of ICT (or programming) by themselves, but cannot necessarily see their possible uses in solving human problems.

The master teacher is one capable not only of instructing but also of constructing a role model for students. Master teachers look for ways to construct learning experiences that are both interesting and appealing to students, something that might provoke and inspire them to attempt to construct something similar by themselves in the hope of reaching the mastery and artistry of teachers, and, perhaps challenging them in the future. In the everyday use of technology, teachers need to be able to get fast and reliable technical advice and have the help of suppliers of technology, technology resource centres, and other teachers and students within the school.

Special kinds of educational support are even more important because they affect the new model of teaching. Such support can be provided both personally and online by a special member of the school staff, by a technology resource centre or university, or by members of the community of teachers using ICT. Different kinds of administrative support are also needed, including an opportunity to participate in ICT events, to buy supplies and use telecommunications, to upgrade technology, and to publicise and promote teachers.

The presence of enthusiastic teachers, together with the installation of hardware and software, add little if support is not present. The introduction of ICT requires establishing and coordinating an entire infrastructure of support. This infrastructure should be multifunctional and include:

i) technical support,
ii) organisational support,
iii) being educational and multilayered,
iv) being present in the school,
v) being present in teachers' and students' homes,
vi) being present in local resource centres and teacher clubs,
vii) universities,
viii) technology providers,
ix) national clearing houses, R&D institutions,
x) international communities and organisations.

Teacher support can involve face-to-face and distance interaction, and all types of workshops and publications (including user groups and bulletin boards). The merging of government, foundations, non-governmental organisations, and informal grassroot efforts is the most effective strategy.

4.2.1. Drawbacks of ICTs

Besides the undoubted advantages of ICT, it is rather important to draw attention to certain drawbacks of ICT.

4.2.1.1. Computer games

Part of the attractiveness of computer games is based on having a feeling of control over a quasi-reality, being in the thick of the action, and the ability to raise self-esteem by achieving goals, power and success in the through-the-screen world (a desire to win, or win back), and a curiosity about the unknown. If something goes wrong, the person in control tries to fix it. In the worst case, this fixing is chaotic and essentially irrational. In that aspect, computer games are similar to other types of hazard games or stock market games. Another dimension of their attractiveness can be associated with purely psycho-physiological mechanisms and a reflexive physiological adrenalin reaction to moving images. Some of this excitement takes place when one is getting accustomed to new software applications, or while creating programmes.

Some programmers may perceive the world and events they are working with in an entirely irrational manner. The process of winning a game, or debugging the programme they create, may depend on the positions of planets or some ritual actions of men! Loss of orientation and the destructive behaviour of a hacker are other negative consequences of ICT use. However, it would be unjust to blame computer-driven information culture for all negative phenomena of contemporary life connected with ICT. The cure for these problems lies not inside ICT themselves, but in building a solid moral orientation for youth in how they use this new information sphere.

4.2.1.2. Unlimited access to information

The advent of ICT has encouraged, in some quarters, a more passive consumption of information, primarily in visual form, which is analogous to the passivity of TV-viewing. We have the mass production of low-quality texts, which are consumed in huge amounts. The internet gives uncontrolled opportunities to publish and more uncontrolled access to such publications. Moreover, it gives children access to pornography and drugs, as well as to child abusers posing as e-pals.

Restrictions have been proposed and introduced, both in families and educational institutions. For example, there are schools where computers do not have floppy-disc drives to prevent students from downloading games (and viruses). There are special internet services, which, if you subscribe to them, will restrict students' access to dangerous and controversial sites on the web. However, these restrictions are really efficient only if students are brought up in an atmosphere of free cultural choice and are encouraged to say no, that is to refuse something of their own accord.

4.2.1.3. Losing traditional skills

Students using computers are less proficient in arithmetic than their friends from non-computerised classrooms, or students of the pre-computer epoch (their parents). A change of priorities in life should influence a change of priorities in education. It is perfectly clear that doing arithmetic mentally or on paper was more important in the nineteenth century than today. Everyone who now does calculations professionally uses a calculator. Many people use calculators while shopping in supermarkets or conducting business negotiations, and especially for calculating tax returns. If you do not use a calculator in a restaurant or supermarket, you will need the ability to add many small numbers and to estimate, not the ability to add or multiply two long numbers. Adroitness in quick and reliable quantitative approximation is more important than the capacity to make pencil-and-paper calculations slowly. The educational consequence of this shift is for less traditional arithmetic in the classroom.

4.2.1.4. Health problems

Working with computers can be more or less effective, it can also be damaging to one's health. The major human organs involved here are eyes and hands. Problems with eyes are caused by concentration on screen images, which are aggravated by unclear or flickering images, by glare, and from bright reflections on the screen. The problem with hand muscles is described as Repetitive Strain Injuries (RSI). In these cases, proper posture, exercises, and relaxation during work are helpful. For students, these considerations are even more important. Other negative factors are excessive heat and noise.

Modern computers need increasingly more processor power for software applications. Fans installed alongside the CPU dissipate the resulting heat, but these produce noise. Another source of noise is the disc drive. High temperature can also cause emission of gases from different components of computers like plastic. There is debate about possible health problems associated with electromagnetic radiation of different frequencies emitted by computer monitors. While there is no evidence of damage caused by the electromagnetic fields of modern monitors, nevertheless, caution is advisable because students are increasingly using computers in schools.

Prior to office machines, accounting clerks used to suffer severe cramp in their hands, which often led to permanent disfigurement. Pianists and other musicians suffer similar ailments from hours of practising, and sometimes promising students are so afflicted that their professional careers are disrupted. Similarly, students with an aptitude for computers may never get to reach their potential because of hours of damaging keyboarding. Video games are doing their share of damage. It is important that potential sufferers are aware that the prevention of RSI may simply require finding a comfortable and efficient posture, and maintaining a balance of movements while working.

Children are generally enthusiastic and become easily infatuated with ICT. They often keep performing an enjoyable task with great concentration until near exhaustion (e.g. making and playing their own animated cartoons for hours with few, if any, breaks). Prolonged activity without regular breaks can cause eye focusing problems (accommodation) and eye irritation. When a student's focusing system is locked in to a particular target and viewing distance, the eyes may be unable to focus smoothly and easily on a particular object, even long after the original work is completed.

Eye irritation may occur because of poor tear flow over the eye due to reduced blinking. Blinking is often inhibited by concentration and staring at a computer screen. Desktop monitors are usually located higher in the field of view than paperwork, resulting in the upper eyelids being retracted to a greater extent. Therefore, the eye tends to experience more than the normal amount of tear evaporation, causing dryness and irritation. Most computer workstations are arranged for adult use and, since children are smaller, computers do not fit them well.

Therefore, students using a computer on a typical office desk must often crane their necks upward further than an adult. Since the most efficient viewing angle is slightly downward about 15 degrees, problems using the eyes together can occur. In addition, students may have difficulty reaching the keyboard or placing their feet on the floor, causing arm, neck, or back discomfort. Students viewing a computer screen with a large amount of glare often do not think about changing the computer arrangement or the surroundings to achieve more comfortable viewing, and this can result in excessive eye-strain.

Inadequate lighting can lead to visual headaches that often occur toward the front of the head, and toward the middle or end of the day. Other symptoms—eyestrain, tired eyes, double vision, and red or dry eyes—are more general. The lighting level for the proper use of a computer is about half as bright as that normally found in a classroom. Increased light levels can contribute to excessive glare and problems associated with adjusting the eyes to different levels of light.

The following are some recommendations for parents and teachers:

i) Have students' vision checked to ensure they can see clearly and comfortably, and to detect any hidden conditions that may contribute to eyestrain.

ii) Limit the amount of time that students can continuously use computers. A 10-minute break every hour will minimise the development of focusing problems and eye irritation caused by improper blinking. Also consider having shorter, more frequent breaks.

iii) Check the height and arrangement of monitors. A student's size should determine how the monitor and keyboard are positioned. In many situations, the computer monitor will be too high in the student's field of view, the chair too low, or the desk too high. A good solution to many of these problems is an adjustable chair that can be raised for student comfort, since it is usually difficult to lower the computer monitor. A footstool may be necessary to support the feet. Monitors should be placed as low as possible in front of students, and notebook computers are preferable to the desktop type.

iv) Check the lighting for glare on the computer screen. Windows or other light sources should not be directly visible when sitting in front of monitors. When this occurs, the desk or computer should be turned to prevent glare on the screen. Draw curtains or blinds to reduce window lighting.

v) Reduce the amount of lighting in the room to match the computer screen. A smaller light can be substituted for a bright overhead light, or a dimmer-switch can be installed to give flexible control of room lighting. In other cases, a three-way bulb can be turned to its lowest setting. Different safety and ergonomic requirements for interacting with computers and other equipment like printers have been developed in different countries. One internationally respected set of requirements has been developed by TCO, the Swedish labour association.

References

Carrucan; Tony, Tony, Crewe, Erica, Matthews, and Matthews, Matthews, *The Internet Manual for Teachers: Access Skills and Curriculum Strategies*, Macmillan Education, Melbourne, 1996.

Clyde, Laurel A., "Yes, but what can we use it for? The Internet in school libraries", *Orana*, 33(2), May, pp.76-89, 1997

D'Ignazio, Fred, "Think intranet", *Learning and Leading With Technology*, 24(1), September, pp.62-63, 1996.

Eade, Jan, "Internet for novices", *Scan*, 15(2), May, pp.56-62, 1996.

Ross, Tweed W. and Bailey, Gerald D., "Creating safe Internet access", *Learning and Leading With Technology*, 24(1), September, pp.51-53, 1996.

UNESCO, *Information and Communication Technologies in Schools, A Handbook for Teachers*, 2005.

5

ICT Integration in Schools

Technology integration is the incorporation of technology resources and technology-based practices into the daily routines, work, and management of schools. Technology resources are computers and specialised software, network-based communication systems, and other equipment and infrastructure. Practices include collaborative work and communication, Internet-based research, remote access to instrumentation, network-based transmission and retrieval of data, and other methods. Integrating technology is what comes next after making the technology available and accessible. It is a goal-in-process, not an end state.

The goal of perfect technology integration is inherently unreachable: technologies change and develop, students and teachers come and go—things change. It is the process by which people and their institutional setting adapt to the technology that matters most. The process of technology integration is one of continuous change, learning, and (hopefully) improvement. Developing a culture that embraces technology is also important to its successful integration; for example, sending important messages by e-mail, or encouraging staff to use electronic calendars to schedule meetings, fosters a culture that accepts technology as "natural" to the business of everyday work.

Standards are valuable in assessing technology integration to the extent that they provide reference points for measurement: rubrics or lists of authentic and observable performances that demonstrate the use of technology in context. Standards set measurable goals for technology integration; they do not assign value positions to the results of measurement. The issue of the desirability of technology integration relates to the links between technology adoption and educational or management outcomes, which are beyond the province of this guide. The lists of observable behaviours can be used by school and district personnel to think about what to measure, and consideration of what to measure in turn leads to thinking about how to measure it.

For the integration standards, teachers can complete coursework, serve as a technology course instructor, prepare a portfolio, or present at a conference. Many resources and training opportunities are available to help employees meet the technology standards, including school-based technology specialists.

The ratio of students to computers is a very poor measure of technology integration in school settings. The goal of placing technology in the classroom is to provide new ways for students to learn. Proper integration of technology will make the technology support these new ways of learning transparently. When students are able to choose and use technology tools to help themselves obtain information, analyse, synthesise, and assimilate it, and then present it in an acceptable manner, then technology integration has taken place.

Establishing and implementing technology literacy standards for students can help guide teacher efforts to integrate technology. There are six categories:

i) Basic operations and concepts.

ii) Social, ethical, and human issues.

iii) Technology productivity tools.

iv) Technology communications tools.

v) Technology research tools.

vi) Technology problem-solving and decision-making tools.

Construction skills are competencies involving the creation and use of non-print texts for developing ideas and opinions, for communicating and collaborating with others, and for enhancing problem solving and personal fulfilment. Construction skills include capabilities for composing, developing, integrating, and presenting. Construction skill competencies (for elementary school students):

a) Use computer-based writing tools to communicate thoughts, ideas, and stories.
b) Use computer-based drawing tools to illustrate thoughts, ideas, and stories.
c) Use digital cameras to illustrate thoughts, ideas, and stories.
d) Use multimedia authoring tools in the creation of knowledge products.
e) Use presentation software in the creation of knowledge products.
f) Use WWW authoring tools in the creation of knowledge products.
g) Use audio tapes for self-directed and/or extended learning.
h) Use videos for self-directed and/or extended learning.
i) Use technology resources for self-directed and/or extended learning.
j) Use technology resources for problem solving.
k) Create nonprint media for personal fulfilment.
l) Explain basic strategies for revising, improving and updating nonprint media.
m) Use telecommunications technologies to participate in collaborative projects.
n) Work collaboratively to seek and/or communicate information in non-print formats.
o) Work collaboratively to create simple non-print information products.

External support that can be used to enhance a person's ability to function within his or her environment, such as advanced voice recognition systems, Braille computer displays, and text-to-speech programmes. Any item, piece of equipment or product system, whether acquired commercially off the shelf, modified, or customised, that is used to increase, maintain, or improve the functional capabilities of children with disabilities.

Technology tool skills:

a) Use advanced features of word processing, desktop publishing, graphics programmes, and utilities to develop professional products.

b) Use spreadsheets for analysing, organising, and displaying numeric data graphically.

c) Design and manipulate databases and generate customised reports.

d) Use teacher utility and classroom management tools to design solutions for a specific purpose.

e) Identify, select, and integrate video and digital images in varying formats for use in presentation, publications, and/or other products.

f) Apply specific-purpose electronic devices (such as a graphing calculator, language translator, scientific probeware, or electronic thesaurus) in appropriate content areas.

g) Use features of applications that integrate word processing, database, spreadsheet, communication, and other tools.

Technology opens up many doors for students at all academic levels to do real work as they study a particular subject. Integrating a curriculum with technology involves making technology into a tool to enhance learning in a content area or multidisciplinary setting. The technology should become an integral part of how the classroom functions, as accessible as all other classroom tools.

Barriers to integration have included inadequate hardware and software, difficulties in securing sufficient funding, inadequate staff development, and deficiencies in planning. It is important to remember, however, that in general the presence of physical hardware in a classroom says little about whether and how it is used in instruction. A "head count" of computers should not be used to answer the indicators below, which are straightforward counts and percentages. Even counting the number of classes set in a computer-intensive "laboratory" setting may be inadequate as a measure of integration, since only technology-specific skills may be taught there.

Instead, measurement should be based on observing actual access and usage. A different sort of technology integration occurs with distance education. Offering courses with a remote teacher provides a school or district with an alternative way to extend the curriculum, and allows several districts to share a scarce or expensive resource. The number of distance education courses offered is an indication of the penetration of distance education into the school's instructional base.

Inclusion of technology in standards general or subject-area (student) standards include items related to proficiency in the use of computer and networking technologies. The school or district has adopted standards for technology proficiency for students, but they are not integrated into general or subject-area standards for teaching and learning. Teacher standards include items related to proficiency in the use of computer and networking technology. The school or district has adopted standards for technology proficiency for teachers, but they are not integrated into general standards for teaching.

Instructional technology should prepare the student for lifelong learning in a rapidly changing technological society by providing a basic understanding of technology usage, processes and systems. This knowledge is necessary for all students regardless of educational or career goals. The Priority Academic Student Skills (PASS) were written to provide utilisation of technology throughout the curriculum. These priority skills were purposely designed to be broad in defining the basic skills for instructional technology statewide. Each level of technology skill is built upon by previous levels. The skills addressed are:

i) operation of the computer.
ii) application software as a tool.
iii) problem-solving skills.
iv) telecommunications skills.
v) ethical and legal issues in technology.

On the one hand, there is interest in knowing if student assessments include measures of technology proficiency or utilisation, whether directly (such as including items in a mathematics test that require use of a calculator) or indirectly (such as an assessment that involved a student presentation done in a computer graphics programme, such as PowerPoint). On the other, there is also interest in knowing to what extent the technologies are used in conducting assessments. The difference, then, is that the second issue is the use of technology in student assessment, while the first issue is the inclusion in student assessments about technology use.

Data-driven decision making can pervade a school or district and lead to continuous school improvement. In all of these areas and more, there is a wealth of opportunities to communicate, and to gain in efficiency by more efficient communication. Computers support the organisation and efficient communication of information; the integration of technology into management involves, at its core, the promotion of efficiencies in sharing information. Although these uses of technology may appear less glamorous than, say, allowing students to point a telescope remotely over the internet, the potential effects of technology in school management are no less revolutionary than in other areas of enterprise management.

Effective integration of technology is achieved when students are able to select technology tools to help them obtain information in a timely manner, analyse and synthesise the information, and present it professionally. The technology should become an integral part of how the classroom functions-as accessible as all other classroom tools.

Change is a process, not an event. Just buying and installing hardware and software is not sufficient to make ICT into a genuine educational technology. This task of implementing ICT in schools demands gigantic efforts, widely time-spread, and covering many diverse but interconnected fields—at the national, regional, and individual school levels. The utmost precautions must be taken not to destroy, or discard anything of value in current practice. On the other hand, we need to be aware of the really deep changes that have begun in education around the world, and which we must direct and manage with care and courage.

The age-old and seemingly endless debates on education reform, so much fuelled by the new digital epoch, gyrate around two diametrically opposed strategies. The first strategy is directed towards a smooth, gradual improvement of the established system, with major repair where needed, and timely replacement of broken or outmoded components and procedures.

This strategy of gradualism stresses the strength of tradition and claims to be a bastion of stability amid a chaotically changing socio-politic and economic environment. In fact, this strategy runs the risk of being an overtly conservative, even reactionary stand that may be vulnerable and shaky in the face of today's challenges and threats. The second strategy requires a drastic paradigm shift from a classical system of education toward a new one built upon totally different principles. This futuristic strategy sees change as its foremost goal, and as a normal part of the life of a school. In breaking all ties with the past, however, the strategy risks impoverishing itself and its students by neglecting the immense riches of our cultural legacy.

There is a third strategy that might be called sustainable schooling. By remaining tradition-conscious and wary of orthodox options, the third strategy is nevertheless ready to make yet another explorative move towards the goals of twenty-first century education. ICT-related reform is essentially a teaching and learning enterprise on a grand scale.

5.1. Stages of ICT Integration

In many countries and educational communities across the globe, attempts have been made to classify various stages of integration of ICT into general education; and then to determine indicators of ICT integration. Several stages of ICT integration in schools have been identified. It is the continuum of stages rather than the actual number of stages that is important:

The earliest stage is the presence of pre-digital (pre-computer) ICT only. The development of information-communicative competence based on these pre-digital forms (photography, using encyclopedias and library resources) and information processing activities with texts and objects of the material world. Following on from this stage, awareness of ICT is based on demonstration of ICT with occasional hands-on experience. A subsequent stage is for some competence in ICT with opportunities to use them for a majority of students and teachers.

Further along the continuum is active and extensive use of ICT in learning and teaching across all subjects in the curriculum. At the furthest end of the continuum, there is transformation of the school in all areas: curriculum, organisational models of work, and relations with the community. What is important to note about these stages of ICT integration is that schools do not necessarily progress through them sequentially. It is quite possible for a school having only a few computers and with only a medium level of ICT-competence among teachers to begin a real transformation in one part of the curriculum, say, in history. Indeed, the normal pattern is for transformation to begin in one area and gradually permeate to all areas of a school's activities.

The most popular indicator for the success of ICT in education today is the number of students per computer, no doubt because it is easily measured. An alternative indicator would be to consider the results of learning. The problem here is that it is much more difficult to evaluate the effects of a "would be" situation, that is, based on a hypothetical reorganised and correspondingly equipped school. ICT is to be effective primarily in those fields and aspects of education that are not central or even non-yet-existing in the traditional school, but vitally important for modern society.

5.2. Dimensions of ICT Development

At all stages of ICT development in schools, across different cultural and economic contexts and across different sized education systems, we can identify certain key dimensions. These include:

i) Leadership and vision

ii) People

iii) Technology

iv) Practice

5.2.1. Leadership and Vision

Encouraging citizens to understand and support change is an important component of any educational reform. In the case of ICT, this support and understanding is even more crucial. A positive attitude and active involvement is needed by all the following groups or stakeholders: national authorities, officials and legislators—to formulate goals and to allocate resources; educational authorities responsible for curriculum matters—to support new systems of educational goals, objectives, and content; school principals—to support their teachers and changes in the life of schools;

a) teachers—to be brave enough to start;

b) parents—to trust teachers; and

c) the general public, journalists, NGOs—to understand and interpret what is happening.

All these groups need their leaders to work inside their sphere of influence and to influence and convince other groups and their leaders of actions in ICTbased educational reform. To do this effectively requires vision. In all successful implementations of ICT in schools around the world, a key dimension is always leaders with a strong commitment for ICT and a vision of how ICT can transform teaching and learning within schools.

5.2.2. People

For an ICT-based curriculum to be successfully implemented, another key dimension is people, which means:

i) Supporting teachers who are willing to change their teaching style, to learn new ways of doing things, to reduce the amount of knowledge they assume their students should memorise, and to encourage students to be independent learners within a collaborative environment.

ii) Incorporating ICT-based learning into teacher preparation and in-service training, relevant for teachers, with components of reflection on their learning and design of their teaching.

iii) Providing a framework in which ICT usage is accepted as an incentive for promotion.

iv) Building up a community of educators to share a common vision and experience.

v) Supporting and rewarding interaction between teachers of ICT and all the school.

vi) Introducing a position of ICT-coordinator.

vii) Using students as appropriate for a technical and intellectual supporting labour force.

5.2.3. Technology

Technology might appear to be an obvious, although expensive, dimension in implementing ICT. Simply, buy computers for schools and sit back and watch for the results. Implementing ICT is a complex issue with many different facets.

For a start, equipment is not limited to computers only. We have already listed many types of technological equipment. There is a broad spectrum of precomputer, or pre-digital technology, worth incorporating within an ICT framework in accordance with our educational goals. Digital devices associated with computers magnify its productivity and effectiveness in school. Too often ICT are thought of as involving computers only.

There is even more misunderstanding about educational software than there is about hardware. The most sophisticated hardware is useless without appropriate software. Investment in technology requires, then, investment in professional or educational versions of software: general applications software, professional applications software, teaching software on CD and DVD, and software systems for the control and management of learning.

The purchase of hardware and software involves also a consideration of:

i) Space, together with furniture, power supply, local networking, and installation.

ii) Maintenance, plus support and upgrade.

5.2.4. Practice

Transforming education means not only changing textbooks and teachers' attitudes, but also altering the prevailing practice in schools, that is, the formal frameworks regulating the educational system. This, then, is another key dimension in implementing ICT in schools. Here are areas of school life that need most to be changed: roles of teachers, administrators and other employees, ICT-coordinators, two teachers in the classroom, certification and promotion; functions of space for learning activities, architectural and construction requirements; access to ICT; consumables and supplies; and forms of learning activities and evaluation: homework via the Internet; project-based learning; distance education; examinations with full access to information sources.

References

Alfassi, A., Using information and communication technology (ICT) to foster literacy and facilitate discourse within the classroom, *Educational Media International*, vol. 37, no 3, 137-148, 2000.

Clarke, L. & Heaney, P., "Author online: Using asynchronous computer conferencing to support literacy", *British Journal of Educational Technology*, vol. 34, no. 1, 2003.

Koivusaari, R., "Cognitive strategies and computer-supported learning environments", *Educational Psychology*, vol. 19, no. 3, 309-116, 1999.

Lanham, R.A., "What's next for text?" *Education, Communication and Information.* vol. 1, no. 1, 2001.

Lankshear, C. and Knobel, M., "New technologies in early childhood literacy research: A review of research", *Journal of Early Childhood Literacy*, vol. 3, 59-82, 2003.

Selwyn, N. and Bullon, K., "Primary school children's use of ICT", *British Journal of Educational Technology*, vol. 31, no. 4., 2000.

Watts, M., and Lloyd, C., The use of innovative ICT in the active pursuit of literacy, *Journal of Computer Assisted Learning*, vol. 20, no 1, 50-58, 2004.

6

Hardware Networking, Software and Connectivity

A new gap is arising between those who have access to and can use modern information and communication technology (ICT) systems and those who lack the access and ability to participate actively in the Information Age. No single solution exists to address the immense challenges of providing quality education and bridging the ICT gap. One possibility is to develop and apply new approaches and strategies for teaching and learning that integrate computers, internet-enabled collaborative learning, and related educational technologies with routine teaching and learning. When used effectively and integrated into education, computers and internet technologies can improve teaching and learning, strengthen teacher professional development, support broad educational reform, enhance school-community partnerships, and improve school management.

These educational objectives by integrating computer and internet technologies into education forces education planners, principals, teachers, and technology specialists to make many decisions about the technical, training, financial, pedagogical, and infrastructure requirements of school computerisation programmes. There is no single best computer configurationor single infrastructure solution to suit all situations. Rather, there are only optimum solutions for each school. Arriving at these optimum solutions is not simply a technical process but requires a careful consideration of educational goals and an understanding of the different costs and benefits, both economic and educational, of different technology options.

To achieve optimum educational results, each school or school system should base infrastructure decisions on an assessment of a mix of technical factors and educational needs and objectives. The results of such an assessment then must be compared to the costs and benefits of a variety of computer system configurations and infrastructure options.

Computers can be distributed in schools in three basic ways to meet educational goals. They can be provided to individual classrooms; installed in central computer labs, libraries, and teachers' planning rooms; or moved from room to room on mobile carts. Each of these options, and combinations of them, has associated benefits and costs that need to be considered carefully to select the options that best meet a school's needs.

Some educational technology specialists argue that proximity and easy access to computers achieved by placing them in classrooms are crucial in achieving high rates of student and teacher use and, thus, educational benefits. Similarly, some people think installing computers in central computer rooms or labs is "old fashioned" and inhibits effective educational use. These are overly simplistic perspectives because the distribution of computers is only one factor in determining how teachers and students use them, and the internet, to enhance teaching and learning.

6.1. Benefits of Computers in Individual Classrooms

One of the greatest potential benefits of distributing computers to individual classrooms is to provide teachers and students with easier access to these educational tools. More specifically, having computers in classrooms can:

i) make it easier for teachers to integrate computer and internet use into routine educational programmes—but this cannot be guaranteed;

ii) allow for spontaneous use of these tools during instructional activities;

iii) permit teachers to organise students into a variety of learning activities, some using computers and others not; and

iv) make it easier to individualise instruction and strategically integrate computer and internet technologies into project-based learning.

Achieving the multiple benefits of classroom-based computers demands significant financial investments to:

i) purchase sufficient hardware and software so that all classes have equal access to computers;

ii) refurbish all classrooms so that there is sufficient room for the computers and a suitable electrical supply, security, networkability, and connectivity;

iii) provide each teacher with a high degree of computer technical and pedagogical skills since education technology specialists will not be available to help as they would in a computer lab; and

iv) supply ongoing technical and educational support.

Unfortunately, not all schools can afford enough computers to enable effective student access and use. As a result, some schools may decide to install only one or two computers per classroom, which likely will have little or no impact on learning. Experience also shows that when there is only a single computer in a classroom, it often becomes the "teacher's" computer and is rarely used by students.

Considerations for installing computers in classrooms include:

i) *Teachers' skills*: Computers in classrooms usually require teachers to have a high degree of technical skill and the capacity to integrate computer use into their teaching.

ii) *Space and student numbers*: Placing clusters of computers in a classroom to enable effective student use requires enough space for both the computer systems and groups of two to three students to sit comfortably in front of the computers, circulation area for teachers and nontraditional student seating arrangements.

iii) *Quality and availability of electricity*: As mentioned above, computers demand a quality electrical supply. Remodeling classrooms to meet the electrical needs of computers is usually very expensive, especially if it needs to be done in many classrooms.

iv) *Security*: Maintaining sufficient security to prevent theft of equipment, software, and supplies, while also enabling open access to the classrooms to a variety of users, is usually impossible.

6.1.1. Maintenance and Support Services

Distributing computers throughout the classrooms in a school makes it more difficult, and more expensive, to provide effective maintenance and support services.

i) *Internet access*: Providing even limited internet access in each classroom via intermittent use of a single dialup phone connection can be expensive, and high-speed access can become prohibitive.

ii) *Connecting computers within the classroom and the school*: Most schools require extensive remodeling to enable computers in classrooms and schools to be connected to form cabled networks. Also, creating classroom networks can require significant investments in additional hardware (servers, hubs, routers, etc.).

Installing computers in classrooms can make it more difficult to provide community access to these costly resources. This difficulty is exacerbated if the number of computers per classroom is relatively low, since no single room may have a sufficient number of computers to meet community use and training needs. As a result, schools with classroom-based computers may not be able to generate enough revenue to cover the costs of consumables, maintenance, and replacement of systems through community access to their computers.

With sufficient funding, and under the right conditions, with highly skilled teachers, classroom-based computers can have a significant impact on the quality of teaching and learning Classroom-based computer installations with low student-to-computer ratios also can provide unparalleled student access to computer use and enable teachers to integrate the use of computers and the internet in ways that cannot be achieved by any other configuration. However, for most schools, especially those in developing countries and poor communities, it isn't possible to install computers routinely in classrooms. Under these more common conditions, alternative strategies must be considered.

6.1.2. Establishing Computer Labs

Establishing one or more computer rooms or labs is a popular way to provide equitable access to computers for the greatest number of users at the lowest possible cost. Computer labs enable schools to concentrate expensive resources in a common space that can be used for student educational activities, teacher professional development events, and community groups. When using computer labs, it is important to arrange computers along the walls of the room rather than in rows facing the front of the room, so teachers can view all the students' work from a common point and move quickly and easily from student to student, providing feedback, support, and guidance. This arrangement also can make it easier and less costly to provide electricity and network access for the computers.

6.1.2.1. Benefits

i) Establishing computers in a lab or dedicated room only requires schools to install quality electricity, network cabling and servers, internet access, effective security, climate control systems, good lighting, and specialised furniture in one or two rooms in a school rather than in many different rooms.

ii) If designed effectively, a dedicated room ensures sufficient space to allow students to work in groups and move about to see each other's work, while also allowing teachers to move from group to group to provide input and guidance.

iii) Computer labs can be maintained by one or two staff members who also can provide technical and pedagogical support to teachers.

iv) Equipment and software can cost less for computer labs used by all classes than for classroom-based systems.

v) Computer labs can optimise return on technology investments if their use is scheduled effectively.

vi) It can be easier and less costly to provide access to the internet via computer labs than with classroom systems since many computers can use a common connection to the internet.

vii) Computer labs can make it easier to encourage collaborative interdisciplinary projects among groups of teachers and students.

viii) Computer labs make it easier to provide community access to computer systems for public relations, and to generate revenue to cover the costs of consumables, internet connectivity, and replacement of old equipment.

6.1.2.2. Challenges

i) Computer labs can become oversubscribed quickly, and competition for use may make it difficult for teachers to engage their students in longer-term projects and activities.

ii) Scheduling conflicts can frustrate teachers and inhibit their use of computer labs.

iii) Once the novelty of using computers wears off, encouraging teachers to move their students to the lab may become more difficult.

iv) Spontaneous need to use computers for research, reference, word processing, etc., can be difficult or impossible to accommodate.

v) In some schools, principals or lab coordinators may implement policies designed to keep the computers safe at the expense of using them.

Schools can overcome many of the challenges of using school computer labs by devising and implementing effective policies governing the use of the labs. A computer lab coordinator is a critical asset and can continue to promote use of the lab and help teachers deal with scheduling conflicts. Labs also can include one or two open- or free-access computers that can be used by students and teachers without scheduling.

6.1.3. Computers-on-Wheels (COWs) Systems

Computers-on-Wheels (or COWs) systems are essentially rolling carts that hold one or more computers (often 10 to 20), usually laptops, often with a printer, and with the possibility to connect the cart to the school LAN via a single classroom network connection. COWs can be brought into a classroom, often by an educational technology specialist, when the teacher wants to use computers for a specific activity. Some of the benefits and challenges of using COWs are discussed below.

6.1.3.1. Benefits

i) COWs make it possible to provide teachers access to computers in their classroom without having to remodel the room significantly, provide special furniture, or reserve space for dedicated computers.

ii) Working in small groups at their desks enables all students to have access to computers even in crowded classrooms.

iii) Using battery-powered laptops makes it possible to avoid providing special electrical power or installing additional power outlets.

iv) Using infrared printing and wireless networking cards enables the students to print their work and connect to each other and the school network for e-mail, electronic communication, and, possibly, internet access without cables.

v) COWs allow schools to optimise the use of expensive equipment by enabling teachers to request a cart of computers.

vi) COWs may be more affordable than remodeling classrooms, building special computer labs, providing special electrical supplies, installing cabling to network all the computers, and buying special furniture.

vii) Since software only needs to be purchased for the computers on the carts, and not for dosens of computers in each classroom, the cost of software can be much less with COWs than with classroom-based installations.

viii) COWs can be stored in secure rooms when not in use.

ix) COWs can provide access to computers in situations where students have classes in different rooms.

x) COWs can be customised to include expensive specialised equipment that normally would not be part of a classroom system.

xi) COWs often are brought to classrooms by an educational technology specialist who can help teachers to make effective use of the computers in teaching and provide immediate technical support.

xii) COWs can be used in teacher professional development programmes.

xiii) COWs can be used to support school-community computer programmes because they can be brought to the room in the school used by community members.

6.1.3.2. Challenges

i) The cost per computer to create a COW system with

laptops and wireless networking capabilities is higher than for conventional desktop computer systems.

ii) There is a greater risk of equipment damage from accidents, hard use, or dropping.

iii) Dedicated staff is often needed to maintain COW systems, deliver them to teachers, and help teachers set up and use the equipment.

iv) Schools with multiple floors and no elevators have to have COWs for every floor or restrict their use to specific floors. The same is true for schools made up of different buildings.

v) The difficulty of scheduling the use of a limited number of COWs may frustrate teachers and deter them from using these systems.

vi) COWs can perpetuate the belief that computers in education should be limited to "special" computer-aided activities.

vii) COWs, especially when used in secondary schools, can limit opportunities for interdisciplinary teaching and learning, since it can be more difficult to bring a mix of teachers and students together in a one-teacher classroom than in a common space.

For schools with few extra rooms for labs and no space or funds to build them, COWs offer a cost-effective way to provide teachers and students with access to computers and internet connectivity. If COWs are used, effort should be made to promote the use of the COWs and to help teachers move beyond simple uses of computers in education. Without added educational inputs, COW systems can fall into disuse and rarely find their way into the classroom.

6.1.4. Computers in Libraries and Teachers' Rooms

When funding and staff resources are scarce, schools can optimise investments in computers and internet access by installing a few computers in public spaces, such as the library or teachers' room. Giving teachers private access to computers and the internet can encourage them to learn to use these technologies and integrate them into their daily routines.

6.1.5. Hybrid Options

Wherever possible, the greatest educational returns on technology investments can result by using combinations of the above configuration options. For schools with sufficient room, suitable infrastructure, and adequate funds and technical resources, distributing some computers to classrooms either as stationary systems or via COWs can be an effective means of easy and spontaneous access. Computer labs then can be used for whole class access and interdisciplinary use. Library computers can be used to focus on research activities, while special classrooms can be outfitted with computers, especially for special-needs students, creating benefits that are difficult to achieve from computer labs. The combination of these different options with one or more computer labs can create an ideal solution to providing students and teachers with access to these rich and powerful educational tools.

6.1.6. Networking

Connecting computers together to form a network, and connecting school, lab, and classroom networks to the internet can multiply the educational value and impact of computers in schools. There are a variety of options for creating classroom, lab, and school computer LANs.

6.1.6.1. Peer-to-Peer Networking

As with all networked computers, users can share files and resources located on computers in the network. With peer-to-peer (see Figure 6.1) networking, however, there is no file server or central computer to manage network activity. One or more of the computers in a peer-to-peer network can provide centralised services such as printing and access to the internet. Most desktop operating systems come with software to enable peer-to-peer networking once the computers are connected by some cable or wireless networking infrastructure.

Peer-to-peer networking is good for small networks where a centralised file server is not needed and network security is not a major issue. This type of networking is less expensive to set up since the only additional expense is in the cables and networking hardware (one or two hubs).

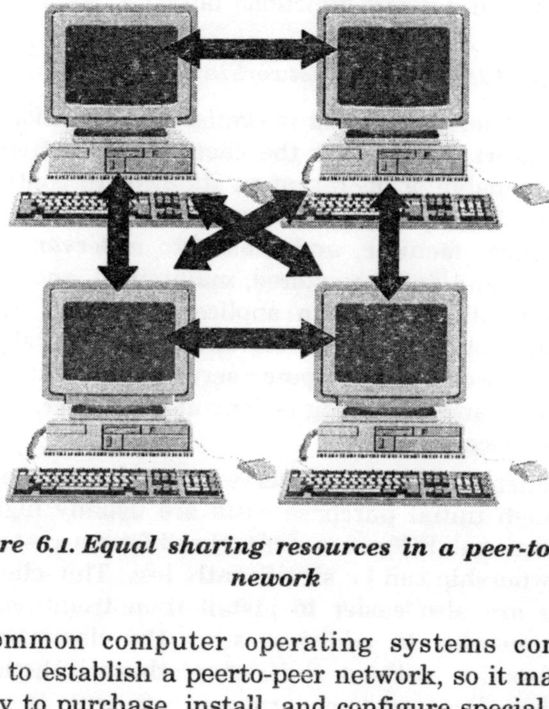

Figure 6.1. Equal sharing resources in a peer-to-peer nework

Most common computer operating systems come with software to establish a peerto-peer network, so it may not be necessary to purchase, install, and configure special network operating system software such as Windows NT, Novell Netware, or Linux.

6.1.6.2. Client/Server Networking

As a computer network grows in size and complexity, it may be necessary to shift to a client/server style of network using more advanced network operating software. One of the advantages of client/server networks is that they are scalable: more clients and servers can be added to the system without changing the network significantly. These centralised networks are easier to manage, administer, and secure than peer-to-peer networks. These benefits come with some disadvantages, however. Due to the need to have a central "dedicated" server, initial costs are higher. Also, they are more complex to set up and maintain than stand-alone computers and peer-to-peer networks, often requiring schools to hire a technician to oversee the network. Also, if the server fails, all network functions fail.

6.1.6.3. Thin-Client/Server Networking

A thin-client/server network is similar to a traditional client/server network except that the client is not a freestanding computer capable of operating on its own. In contrast, thin clients are desktop appliances or network devices that link the keyboard, monitor, and mouse to a server where all applications and data are stored, maintained, and processed. The server, often called an application server, is built to provide all networking services and computer calculations. Since all network and computer services are centralised, all maintenance and upgrading is done at the server; there is no need to service the clients.

Proponents of thin-client/server networks emphasise that even though initial purchase costs are usually higher than with traditional PC/server networks, lifetime costs or total cost of ownership can be significantly less. Thin-client/server networks are also easier to install than traditional client/server networks. In addition, since the client appliances cannot function without the server, there is little risk of theft. Thin-client systems are very efficient at providing access to the internet, and, because the client appliances have few moving parts and limited functions, thin-client/server networks are more reliable and stable than traditional network systems.

A major disadvantage of some thin-client/server networks is that little educational software is written to run on thin-client servers running a version of UNIX. Most of these servers come with special emulation software, but this is usually an incomplete solution: software often runs slower and some applications fail to function. Since many thin-client/ server networks are based on a type of UNIX operating system, skills with UNIX are needed to set up and administer. However, if schools have no staff with these skills, but do have access to the internet, it is possible to have a technician at some remote site administer and maintain the network. This enables a school district to have one highly skilled technician manage thin-client/server networks in several schools, thus reducing management costs further. A careful assessment of total cost of ownership and the availability of technical skills at a school or school system can help planners decide if the thin-client/server network is best for their needs.

6.1.7. Connecting Computers

There are essentially three ways to connect computers to form LANs: cables, wireless, and power line systems.

6.1.7.1. LANs

Installing cabling in older buildings or in schools with thick walls built of brick and cement can be expensive, difficult, and time-consuming. To provide a sufficient number of individual connections for each computer, and to allow for flexible arrangement of computers in a room, many ports and cables must be installed. Each cable connected to a computer must be connected as well to a network hub, an electronic device that controls the flow of network traffic between individual computers and the system's server, usually in clusters of 20 to 30 cables.

Several hubs can be connected together to allow larger numbers of computers to be networked together. Hubs usually are housed in shielded and locked network closets to protect the hubs and prevent people from accidentally rearranging the network cables. Cabled networks provide reliable, high-speed-up to 100 Mb per second-transmission of network traffic. Since cable systems are more common than the other two options, it is usually possible to find firms and technicians with the skills needed to install quality cable LAN systems.

6.1.7.2. Wireless LANs

An increasingly popular alternative to cabled LANs is wireless networks. This type of system does not require cables to connect computers to each other and to the server and shared peripherals. Instead, wireless network adapters (receivers) are installed in all computers that will be part of the network. One or more wireless network hubs/ transmitters are connected to the server, usually by a cable (several wireless network hubs can be connected to each other in a daisy chain). Network traffic is then transmitted by the hub to each computer and to and from the server. Wireless LANs have many advantages:

They can be installed and configured in a very short time, since limited or no construction is needed. They allow for a high degree of flexibility. Computers, especially laptops, can be moved around a room or building, within the range of the network signal, without losing their connection to the LAN. They can be less costly to install and use than conventional cabled systems. They allow schools to create customised LAN systems covering single rooms or whole sections of the school. They also can be mixed with cabled systems to create greater flexibility.

Wireless LANs are not a perfect solution for all environments. The speed of network traffic depends on how many computers are using the hub's bandwidth simultaneously. Distance from the hub and thickness and character of walls between the transmitter and receiver can affect the speed and quality of the network signal significantly. Due to the benefits of wireless LANs and their growing popularity, the technology is improving rapidly, and new standards with higher transmission rates are emerging. Over the next few years, the speed and range of transmission will increase, and reliability and security will improve. Wireless LANs will become an increasingly desirable LAN solution for school computer systems.

6.1.7.2. Power Line LANs

Another alternative to installing special network cables that recently has become a reliable technology for some situations is to use the existing power lines in the school to carry the network traffic. Power line networking (PLN) currently is capable of providing reliable network communication speeds between 250Kbps and 500Kbps for six to 20 network access points. Higher-speed systems, ranging from two to 12 Mbps, are also available. Equipment costs are higher than conventional and wireless networking technologies, but these are expected to fall as technical improvements are made and larger-scale systems become available. In some situations, the costs of using PLN can be less than installing cable or wireless systems.

6.1.8. Accessing Internet

By accessing the internet, computers can become powerful communication devices with many educational applications. A variety of options and technologies should be considered when deciding whether and how to access the internet. If direct connection to the internet is not possible, for economic or technical reasons, students and teachers can still gain simulated access to a selection of internet resources by copying valuable websites to CD-ROMs. Then they can use the CDs to access these sites, thus simulating the internet.

For example, the Rio de Janeiro municipal school system provides schools that cannot access the internet directly with a CD containing a selection of more than 100 Portuguese-language educational websites. The CDs, which are updated periodically, use the same browsers that are used with the internet, so that when internet access becomes available, teachers and students will have no difficulty using this technology. The "internet" CDs also can make it easier for teachers to prepare structured educational activities using websites since they can preview the resources quickly before the class session.

In addition, this approach can focus student inquiry because students can explore the CD's resources but cannot surf freely beyond the scope of the activity or become distracted by non-educational websites. Also, since these internet resources are stored locally, no time is spent waiting for websites to load. Even if internet access is available, a

CD with copied websites can make it easier for students to access internet resources rather than relying on a slow, congested connection.

Dial-up Connection: The simplest and lowest-cost connection to the internet is through dial-up access using a single standard phone line.

A dial-up connection can provide internet access to a single computer (for example, in a lab, classroom, teachers' room, or library) or, by using software on a server, networked computers can share this single connection. However, with a shared connection, access can become very slow, since the total available bandwidth (the total amount of data that can be moved through the network per unit of time) is divided among all the computers sharing the same internet connection. If two or three phone lines are available, these lines can be combined using an analogue router to enable multiple phone line access to an ISP, thus increasing available bandwidth.

Schools can get faster and more reliable internet access by using permanent "dedicated" high-speed connections where they are available and affordable. A variety of dedicated high-bandwidth options may be available to schools, including integrated services digital network (ISDN), digital subscriber line (DSL), terrestrial wireless, digital cable, radio modem, and satellite access, as described below. Several new technologies offer the potential for developing countries to leapfrog earlier generations of equipment to provide connectivity. Terrestrial wireless and satellite technologies offer many advantages because they do not require installation of wireline networks. Satellite facilities also can be installed where communication is needed, even in remote and isolated areas, rather than waiting for terrestrial networks to be extended from the cities.

6.1.8.1. Terrestrial Wireless

Cellular: Cellular telephony has become the first and only telephone service for many people in developing countries, where it may be available much sooner than fixed-line service. In countries such as Côte d'Ivoire, Gabon, Rwanda,

Tanzania, Uganda, Cambodia, and the Philippines, there are now more cellular telephones than fixed lines. If no fixed lines are available, but there is cellular service, a cell phone with a cellular modem can be used to allow access to the internet. For example, the community telecentre in Buwama, Uganda, about 60 km from Kampala, connects to the internet via cellular modem.

However, cellular access is often quite costly, and bandwidth is limited. It is likely to be more practical for short bursts of use for e-mail communication than for surfing the web.

Wireless local loop: Wireless local loop systems can be used to extend local telephone services to rural schools without laying cable or stringing copper wire. Thus, instead of a fixed-line connection, schools would have a wireless link to the telecommunications network. Wireless local loop costs have decreased, making it competitive with copper. Wireless systems enable faster extension to new users than extending wire or cable; they also have a lower ratio of fixed to incremental costs than copper, making it easy to add more customers and serve transient populations.

Wireless is also less vulnerable than copper wire or cable to accidental damage or vandalism. Countries with wireless local loop projects include Bolivia, Czech Republic, Hungary, Indonesia, South Africa, and Sri Lanka. If the telephone company does not provide wireless local loop, schools may be able to install or lease their own wireless links to the internet. Point-to-point fixed wireless, such as microwave systems, can provide high-speed internet access by connecting to an ISP's point of presence (POP). These fixed wireless links may be the least expensive means of getting high-speed internet access if wireline services are not available.

Cordless: Short-range cordless extensions can provide the link from wireless outstations to subscriber premises; the DECT (digital European cordless telephone) technology standard also can allow the base station to act as a wireless private branch exchange (PBX) and reduce costs further. For example, DECT has been used in South Africa to provide links to rural pay telephones and telecenters. However, DECT has very limited bandwidth, making it unsuitable for accessing the world wide web.

Wireless access protocol: This wireless protocol has been developed to make it possible to transmit web pages and other data to cellular phones. It can be adapted for wireless services in developing countries so that internet information can be transmitted to low-bandwidth wireless systems. However, the variety of web content accessible through devices enabled by this protocol is still very limited.

Third-generation mobile services: Third-generation mobile networks are beginning to be introduced in some industrialised countries, and eventually may be made widely available in developing regions. They offer greatly increased bandwidth over existing mobile networks, with the possibility of internet access to handheld devices such as portable phones, personal digital assistants, and small personal computers. However, the capital cost of upgrading existing networks is very high, and the price of access for internet applications may be greater than for other options.

6.1.9. Satellite Technologies

Very small aperture terminals (VSATS): Small satellite earth stations operating with geosynchronous satellites can be used for interactive voice and data as well as for broadcast reception. For example, banks in remote areas of Brazil are linked via VSATs, and the National Stock Exchange in India links brokers with rooftop VSATs. VSATs for television reception (known as TVRO-television receive only) deliver broadcasting signals to viewers in many developing regions, particularly in Asia and Latin America.

Internet via satellite: Internet gateways can be accessed via geostationary satellites. For example, MagicNet, an ISP in Mongolia, and some African ISPs access the internet in the United States via the PanAmSat global satellite system, and residents of the Canadian Arctic use Canada's Anik satellite system, while Alaskan villagers use U.S. domestic satellites. However, these systems are not optimised for internet use, so they may be quite expensive. Also, there is a half-second delay in transmission via geosynchronous satellites, although it is a more obvious hindrance for voice than data.

Interactive access via VSAT: Several companies offer fully interactive internet access via satellite; examples include Gilat, Hughes Gateway, and Tachyon. Systems typically are designed for small-business or home office use, but could be a solution for schools with no other communication options. The price of internet access is likely to decline as new protocols are developed to make more efficient use of bandwidth and, thus, lower transmission costs for users.

Data broadcasting by satellite: Geosynchronous satellites designed for interactive voice and data can be used for data broadcasting as well. For example, the WorldSpace satellite system delivers digital audio directly to small radios. While one market for these products is people who can afford to subscribe to digital music channels, the systems also can be used to transmit educational programmes in a variety of languages for individual reception or community redistribution.

It can also be used to deliver internet content; schools or telecenters can identify which websites they want to view regularly, and WorldSpace broadcasts the data for reception via an addressable modem attached to the radio. WorldSpace has donated equipment and satellite time for pilot projects at schools and telecenters in Africa.

Store-and-forward messaging: Volunteers in Technical Assistance (VITA) has developed a satellite-based system, called VITAsat, capable of delivering sustainable, low-cost communications and information services to remote communities. The system uses simple, reliable, store-andforward e-mail messages relayed to the internet via low earth-orbiting satellites. Using compression technology and software that allows access to web pages using e-mail, VITAsat can make the internet accessible virtually anywhere.

VITA's two current satellite systems have the capacity to serve about 2,500 remote rural terminals that could be installed in schools, clinics, community centers, and NGOs. VITA plans to include local skill and organisational capacity building and development of targeted information content and services designed specifically to meet the needs of small businesses, local NGOs, educators, health workers, and other relief and development workers.

6.1.9.1. Wireline Technologies

Innovations in wireline technology make it possible to provide high-speed internet access over telephone lines, rather than having to upgrade existing copper networks. These technologies may be used in urban areas where basic telephone service is available.

Integrated services digital network (ISDN): Regular twistedpair copper telephone lines can carry two 64 kbps channels plus one 16 kbps signaling channel. One channel can be used for voice and one for fax or internet access, or two can be combined for videoconferencing or higher-speed internet access. Developed in Europe, ISDN may be available from telephone companies in some urban and suburban areas of developing countries.

Digital subscriber line (DSL): Several variations of DSL technology have been developed that provide data rates from 384 kbps or more downstream over existing telephone lines. This technology is replacing ISDN in industrialised countries because of its greater bandwidth. It can be used in urban areas where copper wire is already installed, but its range is limited to about one kilometre from a telephone exchange.

Cable modems: Some cable television systems can also be used for high-speed internet access via cable modems. Like DSL, cable offers much higher bandwidth than dial-up telephone lines. However, a high volume of users may result in congestion of a shared cable network, and older networks may not be converted easily for two-way connectivity.

Optical fibre: Telephone companies upgrading their networks may install optical fibre for institutional customers such as hospitals, schools, and businesses. The advantage of fiber is its enormous bandwidth, which can be used for highspeed internet accessing or other services such as videoconferencing. However, the price of access may be prohibitive. Some schools have managed to gain free or heavily discounted access to so-called "dark fibre," excess capacity that has been installed but is not yet in use.

Hybrid fiber/coax: A combination of optical fiber and coaxial cable can provide broadband services such as TV and highspeed internet access as well as telephony; this combination is cheaper than installing fibre all the way to the customer premises. Unlike most cable systems, this hybrid allows twoway communication. The fiber runs from a central telephone switch to a neighbourhood node; coaxial cable links the node to the end user such as a school. Developing countries with such projects include Chile, China, India, and Malaysia.

Other technological innovations that can be used for educational communication in developing regions include:

i) *Internet telephony (voice over IP)*: Packetised voice communication can be transmitted very inexpensively over the internet. Schools with internet access may be able to use their networks for voice communications as well (regulations vary by country). Using internet protocols for voice and data is much less expensive than using regular telephone networks.

ii) *Community radio*: Small community radio broadcasting stations can be important news sources for the community and can be used to broadcast educational radio programmes for listening in school, at home, or in community centres. Some school and telecenter projects are combining computer facilities with community radio stations, so that information received via the internet can be communicated more widely. Portable windup or solar-powered radio receivers are practical for school and community use.

In addition to choosing a means of connecting to the internet, it also will be necessary to choose an internet service provider (some ISPs bundle connectivity with services). Factors to consider include:

i) *Distance to point-of-presence (POP)*: Ideally, the ISP should provide local connectivity so that long distance calling charges are not incurred. However, in many rural and developing regions, local access is not available. In such cases, it will be important to consider the price charged by telecommunications operators to reach the POP, and whether there are any toll-free or flat-rate options.

ii) *Speed and reliability of access to the internet*: The speed of access to the internet depends not only on the bandwidth available to reach the ISP, but also the number of ports at the ISP and the bandwidth it has available to reach an internet gateway. In addition to asking the ISP for such information, it is useful to check with other customers to determine whether they experience outages or delays, and whether they have noticed any improvement or degradation in access over time.

iii) *Batched and compressed e-mail accounts*: Users can save money in telecommunications charges if they can compose messages offline and send and receive e-mail in batches to the internet service provider (ISP). A batched e-mail service using the compressed UUCP (UNIX to UNIX copy) transfer protocol is four to eight times faster than the standard TCPIP/ POP (post office protocol) used by most e-mail clients.

iv) *Web hosting*: The ISP should provide web-hosting capability if another web-hosting site is not already available in the country. Alternatively, schools can use one of the free web-hosting services made available by some US, European, or Australian sites.

6.1.10. Software for Educational Computer System

Software, an essential component of computer systems, enables the hardware to do useful work for users. Software for educational computer systems is organised into the following four broad categories:

i) operating system (OS) software for client and server computers;

ii) basic computer application software, including software for word processing, spreadsheets, presentations, and graphics;

iii) educational software applications; and

iv) Internet-related and delivered software, including browsers, Java applications, and interactive tools on Websites.

6.1.10.1. Operating System Software

Decisions about what operating system software to use on client or end-user computers are usually based on the type of hardware purchased. If Apple computers are purchased, then Apple's OS, which comes with the computer, will likely be used on client computers. If computers with Intel or Intelcompatible CPUs are purchased, the computers likely will come with a version of the Microsoft Windows OS. In contrast, decisions about what software should be used to operate networked computers are not as easy or predetermined as they are with client system software.

Basic Apple and Windows operating system software comes with the capability to enable computers to be connected together to manage small networks. However, larger and more robust networks that may need to be managed securely will require special network operating system software installed on the network's server to manage the functions of the network, including links to printers and other peripherals, e-mail, file sharing, security functions, and communication among linked computers.

6.1.10.2. Open Source Software (OSS)

For education systems, the education functions that need to be supported and the needs of students and teachers are the most important factors in making technology decisions. If the software and hardware solutions do not ultimately serve the teaching and learning process, then even "inexpensive" or "free" options can be very costly educationally. If key educational software programmes cannot be used on computer systems with "free" OS software, then the "free" solution could become very expensive. Similarly, educational uses and needs for computers are often quite different from corporate needs—and decision making about technology choices for schools needs to reflect these differences.

Linux, part of the family of UNIX-based operating systems, is one of the most popular open source software products used for computer operating system software. Linux has become popular primarily because it is available free of charge and has a large development and user community. Linux is also the first or second most popular operating system software for internet servers—accounting for about 30 per cent of all web servers in the world today. It is used only rarely as a client operating system, however, mainly because few software applications, such as word processing, can be used on computers running Linux. The exception is WordPerfect's and Sun's StarOffice's application suite.

The technical benefits of operating system and network operating system software generally are discussed in terms of the software's reliability, performance, scalability, security, and cost. A variety of comparisons have shown that servers running Linux crash less often and perform better than commercial and other OSS software. Also, Linux can be used on a wider range of computer platforms than any other operating system and is more secure than commercial OSS. Finally, studies have shown that Linux and other open source software usually have significantly lower initial costs than commercial operating system software. Proponents of using Linux in educational computer environments often emphasise the fact that Linux is "free", and that the money saved from not having to purchase operating system or network operating system software is a sufficient reason to use it.

Operating system and network operating system software only account for about 5 per cent to 8 per cent of the total cost of buying a client computer system. In contrast, the ongoing costs to train teachers to integrate technology into teaching and learning, and to support and keep computer systems running from year to year, can be many times greater than the original purchase cost of the computer and the operating system or network operating system software. In many cases, school systems will spend as much in two years for operating school computers as was spent initially to purchase and install a system that is expected to last five years. Therefore, it is more important to consider the total cost of ownership carefully-acquiring, installing, configuring, supporting, maintaining, training users in, using, and upgrading the software—when evaluating the real costs of using different types of operating or network operating system software. It is also important to emphasise that total cost of ownership studies carried out for corporations cannot and should not be used to justify purchase decisions for educational systems.

There are special and critical differences between the needs and uses of computers in education and corporations. The most important factor in realising the potential educational benefits of technology is how teachers and students use computers and the internet in learning activities. Consequently, the most important cost factors in total cost of ownership studies of technology in education are linked to the use of technology and its integration into teaching and learning. Therefore, when evaluating the use of OSS in education, it is essential to assess how different software decisions will affect how teachers and students use technology and how easy or difficult it may be for them to integrate it into routine teaching and learning.

6.1.10.3. Basic Computer Application Software

All computers in schools require a basic set of software applications to be useful for computer literacy programmes and to be integrated effectively into routine education programmes. These applications generally include software for word processing and manipulating numeric data such as spreadsheets, presentation software, and graphics software, and the increasingly important software to create Websites and HTML documents. As with operating system software, commercial and public domain options are available. Major commercial applications often are purchased because they are the types of software used in businesses and government offices, and it is often important to prepare students to use computers and applications that are common in the workforce.

Where funding is a constraint, schools have the option of using Sun Microsystems public domain software application suite, called OpenOffice. It includes an integrated graphical interface similar to MS-Office and WordPerfect and comprises word processing, spreadsheet, and presentation applications. StarOffice also has support for AutoPilot web page design software, 3D graphics, diagrams, HTML editing, and calendar, newsgroup, browser, e-mail and scheduler, photo editing, and other applications. This software is also available in a variety of languages and can be downloaded for free from the internet. There are versions of StarOffice for Windows and Linux operating systems.

6.1.11. Educational Software Applications

Thousands of software applications have been developed over the years, many for free, to meet specific educational objectives, including:

i) strengthening subject matter competence;

ii) providing drill and practice activities for different subjects;

iii) enhancing logical thinking and problem-solving skills;

iv) enriching research and writing activities;

v) simulating complex or dangerous processes that enable students to change variables and visualise how processes are changed; and

vi) providing opportunities for students to extend learning beyond the scope of classroom activities.

As with all uses of computers to enhance and improve teaching and learning, the key to success is not the type of educational software that is used, but how teachers use the software and integrate it into their teaching programmes.

For example, research has shown that when drill and practice software is used without active teacher participation, performance on standardised math tests can go down. In contrast, when this type of software is integrated into a comprehensive set of activities and actively facilitated by teachers, performance on standardised tests can improve. It is commonly believed that the best educational return on investments in computer systems in schools comes from using specialised educational software.

Significant benefits to teaching and learning can be achieved without using any specialised educational software. However, when used effectively by teachers, many excellent educational software applications can enhance the use of computers in education. Achieving these benefits is not guaranteed, and the costs of purchasing often very expensive software must be considered carefully. Selecting software should not be done based on the publishers' promotional materials. Rather, schools and teachers should seek out evaluations of software from other educators to learn the benefits of and possible problems with the software. Numerous websites can provide evaluations of educational software. When evaluating educational software, teachers and schools need to develop evaluation criteria so that purchase decisions are based on objective and subjective measures of educational quality.

One of the most important benefits of internet- and web-related software is that most of it can be used regardless of the hardware and software installed at schools. The "platform independence" of the internet reduces the costs involved in using the internet in education and enhances its benefits. One key area of internet use is access to a variety of internet and web-based software applications, much of it freely available in different languages that can be used by teachers and students in a variety of ways, including:

i) browser and search software that enables students to carry out research on the internet and engage in enquiry-based learning activities using the millions of websites on the internet;

ii) e-mail software that allows users to send and receive communication from other learners and websites;

iii) listserv or e-mail distribution software that allows groups of users to form and communicate easily by e-mail;

iv) Web-based discussion forum software that allows users to engage in ongoing dialogues in which the topics or themes are linked to form discussion threads;

v) interactive web-based publishing tools that allow students and teachers to publish their thoughts, comments, experiences, pictures, suggestions, etc., instantly on web pages;

vi) internet and web-based chat and instant messaging software that allows users to engage in live text-based discussions;

vii) easy-to-use web page construction and publishing tools;

viii) voice and video software applications that allow teachers and students to participate in synchronous audio- and videoconferencing, if sufficient bandwidth is available; and

ix) file storage and retrieval software that allows users to share digital files easily, including documents, presentations, images, data, and music, with other users.

The existence of these online or web-based software applications that enable users to communicate at a distance has given rise to opportunities for collaborative and projectbased learning that were not possible before the internet. Since learning is very much a social activity, the ability to link students and teachers together to form learning communities can significantly enhance learning outcomes and opportunities to develop lifelong learning skills. Another important category of internet-related software includes applications, many of which are freely available, that enable teachers and students to construct and publish web pages and HTML documents on the internet.

References

Andrews, R., "Learning, literacy and ICT: what's the connection?" *English in Education*, vol. 34, no.3, 3-18, 2000.

Angus, L., Snyder, I. and Sutherland-Smith, W., "ICT and educational (dis)advantage: Families, computers and contemporary social and educational inequalities", *British Journal of Sociology of Education*, vol. 25, no 1, 3-18, 2004.

Ormes, S., The use and importance of the internet in literature-based services in children's libraries, *Electronic Library*, vol. 16, no 6, 379-385, 1998.

Plowman, L. and Stephen, C., A 'benign addition'? Research on ICT and pre-school children, *Journal of Computer Assisted Learning*, 19, no 2, 149-164, 2003.

Passey, D. and Rogers, C., *The motivational effects of ICT on pupils*, London: DfES, 2004.

Scrimshaw, P., "Computers and literacy: effeciency, extension or transformation?" *Literacy Today*, no. 25, 10, 2000.

7

Inquiry-based Learning Activities in the Classroom

Inquiry-based learning is a process where students are involved in their learning, formulate questions, investigate widely and then build new understandings, meanings and knowledge. That knowledge is new to the students and may be used to answer a question, to develop a solution or to support a position or point of view. The knowledge is usually presented to others and may result in some sort of action. Research suggests that using inquiry-based learning with students can help them become more creative, more positive and more independent. This is true for all students, including those with special needs who require more individual attention during the process.

Inquiry-based learning improves student achievement. The effective school library programmes that are centres of inquiry-based learning. A school library programme that is properly equipped and staffed can make a difference in terms of measurable gains in student achievement. School library factors alone can account for improvements of 2 per cent to 9 per cent in student achievement. Success with inquiry-based learning often requires a change in school culture. Some schools, individually or as part of a districtwide initiative, have made inquiry-based learning their instructional priority. Studies investigating the implementation of inquiry-based science education, inquiry-based information literacy programmes and other inquiry-based educational innovations have resulted in guidelines for building a culture of inquiry:

i) Administrators in the school or district have a clearly articulated vision for inquiry.

ii) The vision for inquiry is carried forward despite competing pressures.

iii) Two or more champions promote the vision for inquiry.

iv) Resources and space for inquiry are readily accessible.

v) Teachers collaborate and support each other.

vi) Teachers, students and parents trust each other.

vii) Small, interdisciplinary teams of teachers work together.

viii) Problem-solving and investigative skills are valued throughout the school/school system.

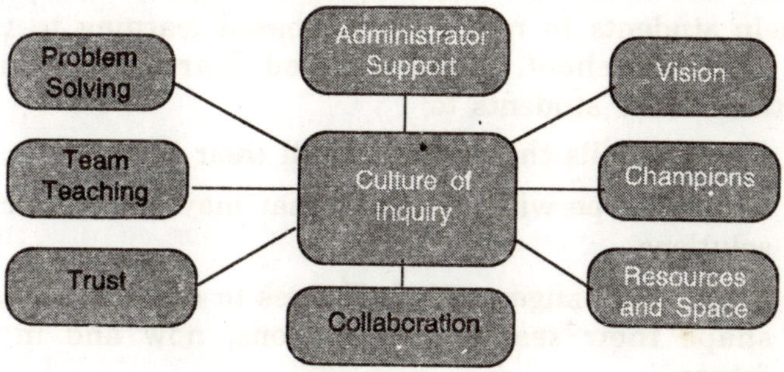

Figure 7.1. Requirements for building a culture of inquiry

7.1. Inquiry-based Learning and Metacognition

Building a culture of inquiry also means recognising, supporting and teaching the role of metacognition. Metacognitive skills are part of the "learning to learn" skills that are transferable to new learning situations, in school and out of school. Through reflecting on the process during inquiry-based learning activities, students are given opportunities to explore and understand both the cognitive and affective domains of "learning to learn". Understanding and dealing with thoughts and feelings makes inquiry-based learning a powerful learning experience for students and teachers.

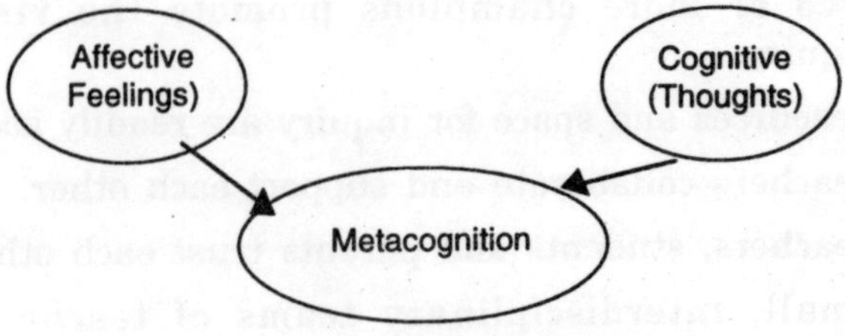

Figure 7.2. Inquiry across the curriculum

The model for inquiry-based learning helps students to internalize a process for inquiry that is transferable to everyday life situations. Thinking about inquiry as a puzzle can help students to relate inquiry-based learning to their lives outside school. Inquiry-based learning provides opportunities for students to:

i) develop skills they will need all their lives

ii) learn to cope with problems that may not have clear solutions

iii) deal with changes and challenges to understandings o shape their search for solutions, now and in the future.

A systematic approach to the development of these skills is essential to prepare students for problem solving and lifelong learning. A systematic approach ensures that students have the opportunity to engage in inquiry, to learn an overall process and to understand that this general inquiry process can be transferred to other inquiry situations. Using these same process skills as they proceed from primary grades through senior high school will enable students to:

i) become familiar with the inquiry process

ii) understand a framework that supports searching for and using information

iii) internalize a variety of inquiry skills and strategies for independent and group use

iv) adapt procedures to various inquiry situations.

7.1.1. Characteristics of Inquiry-based Classrooms

Classrooms where teachers emphasize inquiry-based learning have the following characteristics:

i) Inquiry is in the form of authentic (real-life) problems within the context of the curriculum and/or community.

ii) The inquiry capitalises on student curiosity.

iii) Data and information are actively used, interpreted, refined, digested and discussed.

iv) Teachers, students and teacher-librarian collaborate.

v) Community and society are connected with the inquiry.

vi) The teacher models the behaviours of inquirer.

vii) The teacher uses the language of inquiry on an ongoing basis.

viii) Students take ownership of their learning.

ix) The teacher facilitates the process of gathering and presenting information.

x) The teacher and students use technology to advance inquiry.

xi) The teacher embraces inquiry as both content and pedagogy.

xii) The teacher and students interact more frequently and more actively than during traditional teaching.

xiii) There is an identifiable time for inquiry-based learning.

The Inquiry Model provides the content and structure for instruction-outlining the skills and strategies that need to be taught explicitly in each phase of the process. Referring to the model frequently and consistently during the planning of inquirybased learning activities keeps instructional concerns in the forefront as lessons are prepared and as instructional materials are created. The inquiry process, like any demanding learning experience, brings with it various feelings, including enthusiasm, apprehension, frustration and excitement. These feelings are experienced in a definite pattern in the various phases of the inquiry process. By referring to the model throughout the inquirybased learning activity, teachers are able to anticipate and recognise when students are experiencing strong feelings and are able to design support systems and reflective activities that help students move through the process.

A common language for both teachers and students helps students to internalise the model and to talk about the learning processes involved. It increases effective communication among all inquirers in a school since it gives teachers and students the words to talk about the parts of the process. Posting a model in classrooms and in the library (or any place in the school where inquiry learning takes place) encourages students to recognise each phase as part of the whole process.

The Inquiry Model guides students in using an analytical approach that includes all phases in the inquiry process. Without learning an inquiry process, students often develop a very limited and narrow view of inquiry. They may think that inquiry is finding the answer to other people's questions for the satisfaction of their teacher, rather than understanding inquiry as the process of being puzzled about something, generating their own questions and using information to satisfy their own interests and to develop their own knowledge.

Teachers use the Inquiry Model to assess how effectively students have engaged in the inquiry process, how deeply they understand it, and how effectively the process has been sequenced across grades. For example, a school or district matrix that maps the topics of the inquiry-based units and the skills and strategies introduced, developed and extended across the grades, provides a basis for articulation, coordination and equity. Such a matrix can also be used to balance large-scale and small-scale inquiry activities.

Students can get the experience and practice they need in inquiry-based learning without overloading teachers in a particular grade or subject area. The Inquiry Model is based on more than 30 years of research from around the world, with thousands of children, adolescents and adults in a variety of inquiry settings, and holds true whether the inquirer is a six-year-old, a senior high school student, an undergraduate student at university, a lawyer, a teacher or a researcher.

7.1.2. Phases of the Inquiry Model

The following are the phases in the Inquiry Model:

i) Planning

ii) Retrieving

iii) Processing

iv) Creating

v) Sharing

vi) Evaluating.

7.1.2.1. Planning phase

Inquirers should understand that the underlying purpose of inquiry-based learning projects is to develop their "learning to learn" skills. Inquiry-based learning begins with the inquirers' interest in or curiosity about a topic. It is the puzzle that needs to be solved. At this phase of the inquiry process-the most important phase of the whole process-inquirers often experience a sense of optimism about the tasks ahead. Once students are interested in a broad topic or theme, they need to be involved in:

i) determining what questions will be investigated

ii) how they might find the information they need about a particular topic

iii) how to present information to a particular audience
iv) suggesting criteria for evaluating their research product and process.

7.1.2.2. Retrieving phase

Inquirers may need to spend considerable time exploring and thinking about the information they have found before they come to a "focus" for their inquiry. This pre-focus phase is at first enjoyable for students, as they actively search for information related to their topic. But as the amount of resources they find increases, students sometimes "tune out" and stop searching, since they may not know how to handle the irrelevant data or cannot find the data specific to their inquiry. Since many students are set in what they want to find out, they often become frustrated at this point in the process. Teachers help students past these feelings of frustration by teaching them that these feelings are ones that all inquirers experience, and by teaching them the skills and strategies for selecting relevant information and for adjusting and modifying inquiries.

7.1.2.3. Processing phase

This phase begins when the inquirer has found a "focus" for the inquiry. A focus is the aspect of the topic area that the inquirer decides to investigate. Coming to a focus can be very difficult for students, as it involves more than narrowing the topic. Inquirers usually experience a sense of relief and elation when they have established a focus for their inquiry. Even so, choosing pertinent information from resources is often a difficult task; there may be too little information or too much information, or the information may be too superficial or too indepth for the inquirers. Often the information that is found is confusing and contradictory, so students may feel overwhelmed.

7.1.2.4. Creating phase

Organising the information, putting the information into one's own words and creating a presentation format are the next tasks in the process. Students feel more confident at this phase and want to include all their new learnings in their product, resulting in too much information.

7.1.2.5. Sharing phase

If students have been given enough supports throughout the inquiry process, they are proud of their product and eager to share it, regardless of the format or audience. They may feel a bit nervous about presenting something in which they take such ownership, and they may feel anxious that others may not understand or appreciate their efforts.

7.1.2.6. Evaluating phase

Finally, when a research project is complete, inquirers feel relieved and happy. They are excited about their new skills and understandings, and they want to reflect on the evaluation of their product and their inquiry process. In order to make sense of the inquiry process, they need to understand and question the evaluation criteria, to identify the steps in their inquiry process, and to share their feelings about the process. Students should be able to articulate the importance of this kind of work for developing their "learning to learn" skills, and they should be able to see the connections between their inquiry work done in school and their work or activities that are done outside of school. They should also be able to reflect on how their experience has influenced their personal inquiry model and on what they have learned about themselves as inquirers.

7.2. Inquiry-based Student Learning Outcomes

Teachers recognise the commonalities of curricula across grades and subjects, particularly in the specific outcomes related to skills and attitudes. Inquiry-based learning projects that are integrated with the curriculum and that are cross-disciplinary benefit students by reducing the time required for achieving these outcomes. Inquiry-based student learning outcomes occur in all curricula and grades. Although self-contained "research projects" may be described as inquiry projects, the term "inquiry" has a larger meaning than research. It encompasses the habits of mind that promote learning and the processes that can be woven through all classroom activities to enable students to broaden and deepen their understanding of the world. Inquiry processes begin and are sustained by student curiosity. Inquiry-based instruction fosters and sustains an attitude of inquiry that connects with lifelong learning and metacognition.

The most successful curriculum inquiry projects emerge from topics that are of personal interest to the students. In a teacher-directed inquiry project, students need to have a choice of topics about which they truly wonder and care, and there needs to be an identifiable time when students work on their inquiries, rather than inquiries being what they do virtually all day. In student-directed inquiry projects, the teacher may provide curriculum-related themes and allow students to generate their own topic questions. Therefore, teachers need to use the latest version of curriculum documents to ensure that they have the fullest and most current information in relation to the inquiry-based outcomes for each programme of studies.

7.2.1. Inquiry Activities

The Planning Phase of inquiry is the key to success for teachers, who develop the lesson plans for the inquiry activity, and for students, who are involved in the inquiry. Teachers who plan successful inquiry-based learning activities take the time to think through the process. This planning determines the success of an activity and cannot be overemphasized. In designing an inquiry activity, teachers also follow their own inquiry process. Inquiry-based learning requires many skills and strategies and a wide range of resources from beyond the school library and classroom. It is important that teachers select a curriculum theme that is worthy of the time and effort involved and that will be interesting to students for more than a short-term period. Early selection of a theme and inquiry activity will give teachers the time to build the students' background knowledge, to develop the inquiry skills and strategies that students will need, and to acquire or add to the required resources.

Students learn inquiry skills, strategies and processes more readily when inquiry-based learning activities are:

i) integrated with curriculum.
ii) taught with the focus on developing lifelong learners and critical thinkers.
iii) viewed by students as relevant to their needs.
iv) related to the students' past experiences.
v) shared through cooperative learning.

To help students develop an understanding of the inquiry process, the teacher(s) and/or teacher-librarian:

i) identifies a curriculum entry point
ii) designs an inquiry-based learning project/activity o supports students as they generate and refine a topic o models the process out loud to help students.

As students work through the inquiry process, the teacher(s) and/or teacher-librarian:

i) motivates students to locate, analyse and use information.
ii) assists students to clarify thinking through questioning, paraphrasing and talking through tasks.
iii) provides students with opportunities to record information.
iv) provides students with opportunities to focus on steps required to complete their inquiries.
v) individualizes teaching.
vi) evaluates student progress in content and process areas.
vii) models inquiry behaviours (e.g., demonstrating and modelling the inquiry-based learning process)
ix) facilitates and models questioning behaviours (e.g., providing opportunities for students to develop and ask questions).

If your school has developed a school-wide plan so that all students can experience inquiry-based learning activities throughout their school career, then consult this plan first. School plans vary the content areas and ensure that students are learning, practising and improving their inquiry skills and strategies as they progress through the grades. If your school has not yet developed a school-wide plan for developing student inquiry skills and strategies, begin with the programmes of study, which all have inquiry-based outcomes, and select an area that will intrigue and interest both you and your students.

The teacher-librarian brings to the activity expertise in inquiry-based learning, resource selection, Web site selection and evaluation, and, most importantly, strategies for integrating information literacy skills into the inquiry. Integrating inquiry-based learning activities into the curriculum evolutionary. For teachers who are new to integrating inquiry activities, begin slowly. As teachers and students experience positive development in teaching methods and skills, their commitment to inquiry will increase. The ideal situation for developing an inquiry unit occurs when team teaching or cooperative planning occurs between a teacher-librarian and teacher or between teachers.

7.2.2. Cooperative Planning

Cooperative planning of an inquiry activity involves a teacher working with a teacher-librarian, or teachers working together. The first step is to set out objectives for the inquiry and plan the activities with the teacher-librarian or other teachers. The teaching of inquiry and information literacy skills should be integrated into the plan. Cooperative planning allows for variations in group size (e.g., whole class, two teaching groups, small groups).

Before implementing inquiry-based learning activities with students, plan for the monitoring and assessment of the inquiry process and the final product(s). Planning for assessment provides the foundation for thinking about what students already know, what they need to know, what instructional emphases will be given and what students will have learned when the inquiry activity is complete.

Introduce the inquiry activity to the class as an integral part of classroom studies.

i) Keep a list of questions, issues and problems that arise during the unit for further investigation.

ii) Spread the inquiry activity throughout the unit so that students have time to think about a topic of interest, talk to parents and other family members, and find a focus.

During and after the inquiry activity, record those strategies that were most and least effective. Learning is enhanced when:

i) assessment strategies match the learner outcomes and are aligned to instruction

ii) assessment is integrated with instruction (unit and lesson planning)

iii) assessment relates new concept(s) to previous learning

iv) students are involved with their own assessment

v) students get immediate, meaningful feedback

vi) students of all abilities are able to demonstrate what they

vii) know and what they can do

viii) assessment engages and motivates students.Teachers need to plan for diagnostic, formative and summative assessment when designing inquiry activities.

Inquiry-based learning assessment focuses on the inquiry process to monitor student progress and learning. Ongoing, formative assessment helps teachers to identify the development of students' skills and strategies and to monitor students' planning, retrieving, processing and creating skills during the inquiry activity. This ongoing assessment allows teachers to modify instruction, adapt the inquiry activity and support students with special instructional needs.

The developmental level of the students will have an impact on the nature of an inquiry-based learning activity, the end product and how it is shared. At all levels, appropriate positive feedback and support is necessary for student ownership of the activity. The following factors may be useful for teachers who are implementing inquiry-based learning:

7.2.2.1. For students new to inquiry

a) Students choose from teacher-selected, concrete topics.

b) Students begin work on the project by relating it to their personal experiences.

c) Teacher provides carefully selected resources, including internet sites, for students.

d) Students talk to others, using appropriate protocol, to gather information about their topic.

e) Students are specifically taught skills for reading simple informational texts.

f) Students are specifically taught note-taking skills to record their information, using a graphic organiser that is provided by the teacher.

g) Students begin to use technology to locate, organise and create presentations.

h) Students create a basic report or presentation based on specific guidelines.

i) Students share their final report/project with small groups within the classroom and with family.

j) Students talk about their feelings and progress each class.

k) Teacher identifies and shares evaluation criteria for the process and the product.

l) Students can play a role in setting evaluation criteria for the process and the product.

m) Students understand evaluation criteria for the process and the product.

n) Teacher monitors progress at the end of each class.

o) Students talk about what went well and what was challenging.

7.2.2.2. For students with limited inquiry experience

a) Teacher provides carefully selected resources, including internet sites, for students and also encourages and supports student searches.

b) Students talk to others, using appropriate protocol, to gather information about their topic.

c) Students are specifically taught skills for reading more complex informational texts.

d) Students are taught basic search engine strategies for the internet, including how different search engines work.

e) Students begin to use finding guides, such as online library catalogues, online subject directories, keyword and subject searches, indexes, tables of contents, and databases.

f) Students are taught note-taking skills, using graphic organizers provided by the teacher.

g) Students create a basic report or presentation based on specific guidelines. Students are encouraged to be creative in their product.

h) Students use technology to locate graphics and media to enhance their presentations and reports.

i) Students share their final report/project with small groups, with other classes and with family.

j) Teacher identifies and shares evaluation criteria for the process and the product.

k) Students can play a role in setting evaluation criteria for the process and the product.

l) Students understand evaluation criteria for the process and the product.

m) Students learn and apply appropriate peer-evaluation skills.

n) Students talk about their feelings and progress each class.

o) Teacher monitors progress at the end of each class.

p) Students talk about what went well and what was challenging.

7.2.2.3. *For students with more inquiry experience*

a) Students, with guidance, select issues-based topics (arguing for or against or both for and against) within a general curriculum theme selected by the teacher. Students build on their general background understandings of the theme.

b) Students carefully select and evaluate a variety of resources.

c) Students develop indepth understanding of the topic based on an information retrieval plan.

d) Students work with others to monitor understandings of the topic and sensitivities to the topic.

f) Students are specifically taught skills for reading and evaluating complex informational texts.

g) Students use finding guides appropriately.

h) Students use the internet, with guidance and instruction from the teacher.

i) Students are specifically taught interviewing skills that consider the appropriate protocol for each situation.

j) Teacher provides a choice of notes or graphic organizers for students to record information.

k) Students are specifically taught note-taking skills, including highlighting techniques.

l) Teacher assists students in modifying and adapting their topics.

m) Students create a report or presentation based on guidelines provided in the planning phase and in response to the needs and interests of the intended audience.

n) Students use technology appropriately to enhance their presentations and reports.

o) Students share the final report/project with larger groups, with other classes, in the community and/or with family.

p) Teacher identifies and shares evaluation criteria for the process and the product.

q) Students can play a role in setting evaluation criteria for the process and the product.

r) Students understand evaluation criteria for the process and the product.

s) Students learn and apply appropriate peer-evaluation skills.

t) Students share their feelings and progress each class.

u) Teacher monitors progress at the end of each class.

v) Students talk about what went well and what was challenging.

7.2.2.4. For students who are advanced inquirers

a) Students select specific topics (e.g., issues-based, cultural, comparative, informative, historical, current events, biographical) within parameters set by the teacher.

b) Students develop and support a position or point of view for thesis-based inquiry, which may involve social action that meets community standards.

c) Students build on their general background understandings of their topic to develop an indepth understanding of the topic, based on their own information retrieval and processing plan.

d) Students carefully select and evaluate a variety of resources.

e) Students work with others to monitor understandings of the topic and sensitivities to the topic.

f) Students are specifically taught, as needed, skills for reading and evaluating complex informational texts.

g) Students use finding guides appropriately.

h) Students use the internet, with guidance and instruction.

i) Students conduct interviews in an appropriate and ethical manner (including consideration of privacy and confidentiality).

j) Students record information using the most appropriate note-taking strategies.

k) Students create a report or presentation based on guidelines developed in the planning phase and in response to the needs and interests of the intended audience.

l) Students use technology appropriately and creatively to enhance their presentations and reports.

m) Students share their final report/project with larger groups, with other classes, in the community and/or with family.

n) Teacher identifies and shares evaluation criteria for the process and the product.

o) Students are involved in setting evaluation criteria for the process and the product.

p) Students provide appropriate self-evaluation and peer evaluation of the final product and the inquiry process.

q) Students monitor and adapt their own inquiry skills and strategies during the process.

r) Students share their feelings and progress each class.

s) Teacher monitors progress at the end of each class.

t) Students talk about what went well and what was challenging.

REFERENCES

Alberta Education, *Focus on research: A guide to developing students' research skills*, Edmonton, AB: Alberta Education, Retrieved July 12, 2004.

Drayton, B., & Falk, J. K., "Tell-tale signs of the inquiry-oriented classroom", *NASSP Bulletin,* 85(623), 24–34, 2001.

Fullan, M.G., *The new meaning of educational change* (2nd ed.), New York, NY: Teachers College Press, 1991.

Galiieo Educational Network, What is inquiry? *Inquiry & ICT,* 2004.

Hacker, D.J., "Metacognition: Definitions and empirical foundations", *The MIT encyclopedia of cognitive sciences,* 1999.

Kuhlthau, C. C., & D. Oberg (Eds.), *Inquiry-based learning: Lessons from Library Power* (pp. 13–30).

Worthington, OH: Linworth, Jonassen, David H., *Computers as mindtools for schools: Engaging critical thinking* (2nd ed.), 2000

8

Classroom Learning (1-12) Assessment

Teachers play a central role in the assessment and evaluation of student learning. Technology is defined as "the processes, tools and techniques that alter human activity ... the employment of tools, machines, materials and processes to do work, produce goods, perform services or carry out other useful activities." The Information and Communication Technology (ICT) competencies outlined in the ICT programme of studies are basic life skills for a digital world that enable students to function in a knowledge-based economy and an information-rich society. These skills are no longer optional or complementary. They are an essential component of a student's preparation for life and the world of work.

The ICT curriculum is not intended to stand alone, but to be integrated within the programmes of study for language arts, mathematics, science and social studies. Selected ICT outcomes are blended with core learner outcomes within a common context, such as a project, lesson or activity. The long-range goal is for ICT learner outcomes to be included and contextualised within core and other programmes of study. The Information and Communication Technology Programme of Studies articulates a set of learner outcomes to be achieved over 12 grades of schooling. In making decisions about instructional planning and assessment, these outcomes:

i) are sequenced for each of the four divisions (Grades K-3, 4-6, 7-9 and 10-12).

ii) can be placed into a scope and sequence that specifies which outcomes are taught in particular courses and grade levels.

iii) may be introduced at any time within the division, but are to be achieved no later than the third, sixth, ninth and twelfth grade levels, respectively are to be assessed and evaluated within the language of learning can be assessed and evaluated formatively or summatively when ICT learner outcomes and other learner outcomes remain separate but are part of a common assessment task.

iv) can be reported to students, parents and others as separate marks are to be assessed and evaluated formatively and summatively when ICT learner outcomes are included and contextualized within core or other programmes of studies.

v) are to be reported to students, parents and others as part of the subject mark.

Figure 8.1 illustrates the relationship between the ICT programme of studies and other programmes of study.

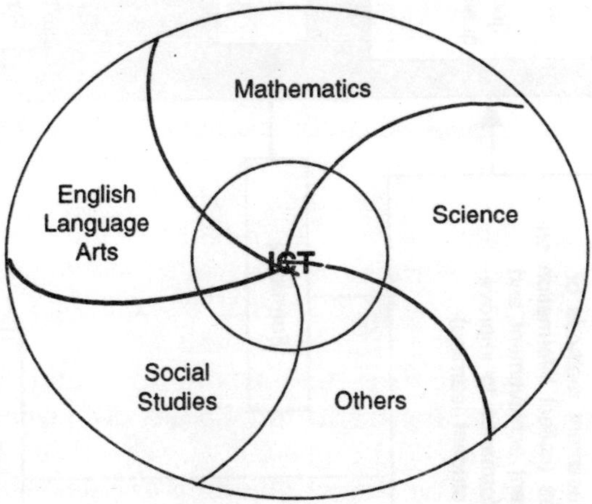

Figure 8.1. Relationship between the ICT programme of studies and other programmes of study

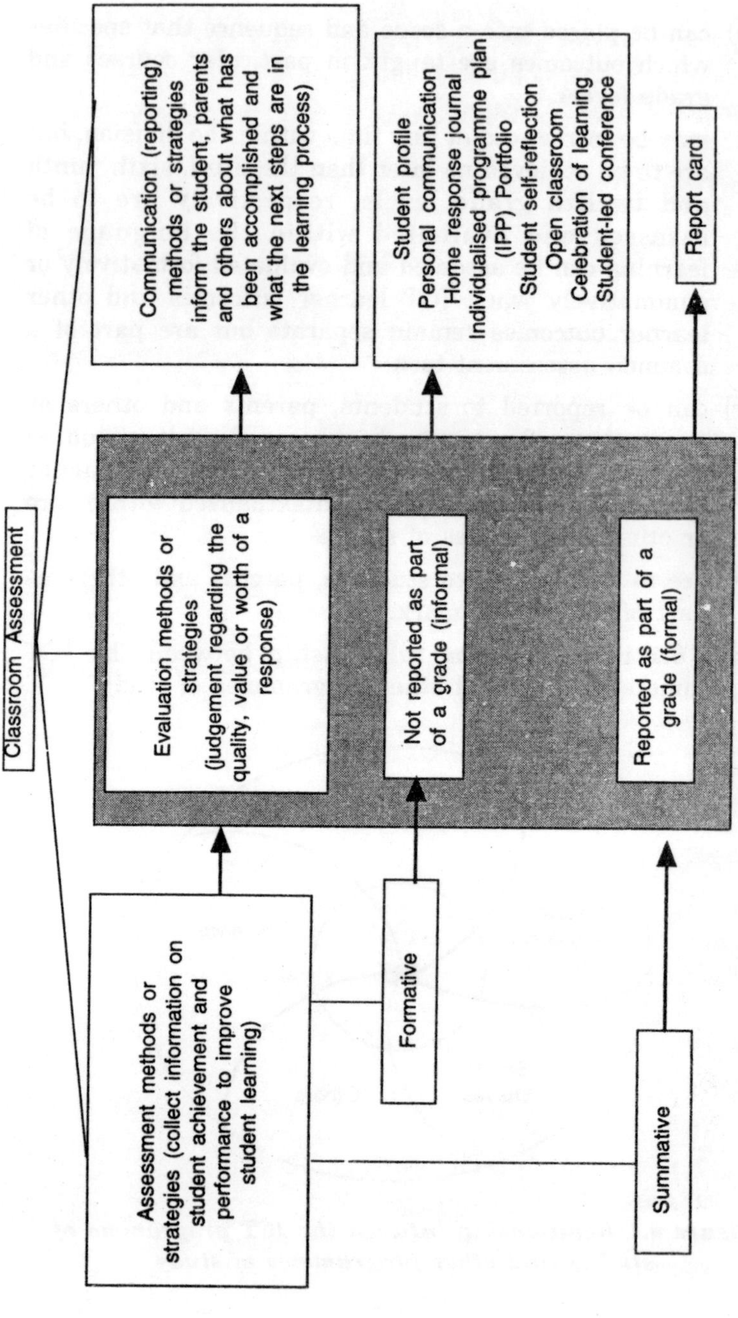

Figure 8.2. A general model of classroom assessment

Figure 8.2, is a general model of classroom assessment that shows the relationship between assessing, evaluating and reporting student learning.

8.1. Growth, Evaluation and Communication of Student Achievement

Assessment, evaluation and communication of student achievement and growth are essential parts of the teaching and learning process. Each part of the teaching and learning process should be a positive experience for students and promote personal growth. Practices should be carried out in such a way that they support continuous learning and development. To assist students in meeting the aim of the ICT programme of studies, assessment should be a continuous, collaborative and comprehensive process that includes clearly identified and communicated criteria. The following principles are essential for effective assessment and evaluation of ICT learner outcomes:

i) *Principle 1*: Assessment should be continuous.

ii) *Principle 2*: Assessment should be collaborative.

iii) *Principle 3*: Assessment should be comprehensive.

iv) *Principle 4*: Assessment should include criteria.

8.1.1. Principle 1: Assessment should be continuous

Assessment practices should be carried out in such a way that they support and enhance ongoing student learning and development. Assessment practices should:

i) require demonstration of both core subject and ICT learner outcomes.

ii) promote student learning.

iii) be part of instruction in a variety of contexts, using varied methods and instruments that match learner outcomes.

iv) be part of an ongoing process rather than a set of isolated events focus on both process and product.

v) provide information about students' prior learning.

vi) provide ongoing feedback about the effectiveness of instruction.

vii) enable students to demonstrate their knowledge and skills.

viii) provide opportunities for students to revise their work in order to set goals and improve their learning.

ix) provide a status report on how well students can demonstrate learner outcomes at that time.

8.1.2. Principle 2: Assessment should be collaborative

Students benefit when they are involved in the assessment process. Assessment practices should help and encourage students to:

i) be responsible for their own learning and develop a positive attitude toward the use of technology in meaningful, real-world situations.

ii) be involved in establishing criteria for evaluating their products or performances—work together to learn and achieve outcomes.

iii) feel competent and successful using technology—set goals for further improvements.

8.1.3. Principle 3: Assessment should be comprehensive

Assessment practices should address learner outcomes and include a variety of strategies that meet the diverse learning needs of students. Assessment practices should:

i) be developmentally appropriate, age-appropriate, genderbalanced, and consider students' cultural and special needs .

ii) be constructive, build on student strengths, and encourage further learning by creating positive atmospheres and self-images.

iii) enable students to demonstrate ICT proficiencies:

— in many different contexts and subjects.

— in meaningful, real-life situations.

— enable students to demonstrate that ICT proficiency is transferable across contexts and subjects.

— include multiple sources of evidence (formal and informal).

— provide opportunities for students to demonstrate what they know, understand and can do.

8.1.4. Principle 4: Assessment should include criteria

Assessment practices should identify and clearly define the critical aspects of performance for demonstrating student learning. Assessment practices should:

i) involve students in identifying and/or creating criteria

ii) communicate the criteria used to evaluate student work before students begin tasks so they can plan for success.

iii) provide students with rubrics to indicate performance levels.

iv) be communicated to students so that they understand expectations related to learner outcomes.

Achievement is based on demonstration of learner outcomes rather than comparing one student's performance to another's. Comparing one student's proficiencies to another's does not motivate students to achieve and frequently has the reverse effect. Meaningful, relevant and realistic criteria for achieving learner outcomes can motivate students to take responsibility for their own learning and develop a lifelong desire to use technology wisely.

A good assessment instrument can be a learning experience. But more to the point, it is extremely desirable to have assessment occur in the context of students working on problems, projects or products that:

i) genuinely engage them

ii) hold their interest

iii) motivate them to do well.

8.2. Performance Assessments

The following are suggestions for developing and using performance assessments.

i) Collect examples of performance assessment tasks and rubrics.

ii) Have ongoing discussions with colleagues about assessment tasks and rubrics—what's working and what's not.

iii) Work with others in your school or department to develop common language about assessments and grading.

iv) Develop a plan of action for including more products or performances in your assessment programme.

v) Add one self-reflective activity during the week.

vi) Add one performance assessment with criteria and scoring rubric per grading period.

When developing performance assessments, begin by selecting subject and ICT learner outcomes. Three to five learner outcomes for each is an appropriate goal. Once students have completed a task, they should be given an opportunity to reflect on their performance and set goals for future learning. This allows teachers and students to link assessment results to teaching and learning.

8.2.1. Student Self-reflection

Continual self-reflection throughout performance assessment enables students to assess progress, identify areas of difficulty, define learning and reassess goals. Self-reflection is the key to continued, powerful learning. As teachers move about classrooms during the administration of performance assessments, they should:

i) provide continual feedback to students

ii) observe student progress

iii) encourage students to continuously self-assess and assist students with difficulties.

Students could reflect on their progress, their learning, what they did not understand, what comes next or changing goals. Information and communication technology learner outcomes can be assessed formatively or summatively. Effective communication informs students, parents and others about the outcomes accomplished and the next steps in the learning process. Communication of student learning should:

i) celebrate and improve learning

ii) enhance the home and school partnership

iii) involve a variety of strategies

iv) reflect a school's philosophy about learning

v) be based on curriculum outcomes.

Information on student progress is required for reporting clearly to students, parents and others. This information is essential in order for teachers to change or refine instructional plans to ensure learning activities are appropriate for all students. The information is also required to evaluate programme effectiveness and revise programmes to improve student learning.

References

Davies, Anne, *Making Classroom Assessment Work.* Merville, BC: Connections Publishing, 2000.

Eisner, Elliot W., "The Uses and Limits of Performance Assessment", *Phi Delta Kappan* 80, 9, pp. 658–660, 1999.

Gardner, Howard, *Multiple Intelligences: The Theory in Practice*, New York, NY: BasicBooks, 1993.

Gregory, Kathleen, Caren Cameron and Anne Davies, *Knowing What Counts, Book Two—Self- Assessment and Goal Setting: For Use in Middle and Secondary School Classrooms*, Merville, BC: Connections Publishing, 2000.

Guskey, Thomas R. "Reporting on Student Learning: Lessons from the Past—Prescriptions for the Future". In Thomas R. Guskey (ed.), *Communicating Student Learning: 1996 ASCD Yearbook*, pp. 13–24, 1996

Jonassen, David H., Kyle L. Peck and Brent G. Wilson, *Learning With Technology: a constructivist perspective*, Upper Saddle River, NJ: Prentice Hall, 1999.

Popham, W. James, *The Truth About Testing: An Educator's Call to Action*, Alexandria, VA: Association for Supervision and Curriculum Development, 2001.

Stiggins, Richard J., *Student-Involved Classroom Assessment (Third Edition)*, Upper Saddle River, NJ: Prentice-Hall, Inc., 2001.

Stix, Andi, *Strategies for Student-Centered Assessment*, New Rochelle, NY: The Interactive Classroom, 1996.

Wiggins, Grant and Jay McTighe, *Understanding by Design*, Alexandria, VA: Association for Supervision and Curriculum Development, 1998.

9

ICTs in Elementary and Secondary Education

Many secondary and even elementary schools today have a computer (or ICT) teacher, and an increasing number of elementary schools also have a person who supervises the computer labs (classrooms equipped with computers). In some cases, this person is a certified teacher. In other cases, the lab supervisor is considered a technical support person and may not be a certified teacher. The technology coordinator position was proposed in the late 1980s to designate an educator at the school or district level who works to facilitate, assist, and consult on the effective use of a wide range of computer-based and digital-related ICT in teaching and learning. This person may also have duties as a non-ICT classroom teacher or as an ICT teacher proper.

Another person who can be useful in introducing ICT is a pedagogical advisor (e.g. another teacher), who can help with relevant lessons and in their preparation. In this case, the elementary school teacher learns hands-on how to use technology in new ways of teaching. With adequate financial support, this can be done on a regular basis, formalising the two-teacher model.

The role of advisor with this responsibility can be held by a technology teacher, a subject-area teacher, a member of a technology resource centre or inservice support institution, university professors and students, or even by a student from the same school. Out of these experiences, general categories of participants can be discerned who support and promote ICT usage in school:

i) *The ICT-using, ICT-literate educator*: Library media specialists fall into this category.
ii) *The ICT teacher*: This person may teach computer applications, hypermedia literacy, programming languages, and computer science to both students and teachers, taking part in group work with other teachers and in interdisciplinary projects.
iii) The technology coordinator.
iv) The pedagogical adviser.
v) Certain students.

School administrators are more accepting of ICT in a school, when they use it themselves. Therefore, provision should be made for this. Moreover, information space of school management should be integrated with learning and teaching space. Information space should be accessible via telecommunication channels to students, teachers, administrators, parents and other members of the local community. Of course, there should be limitations on access and authority to change information.

A school's ability to use ICT is based on the ability of its teachers. At the same time, most decisions are made at a higher level of administration, where money is allocated for school needs. Naturally, some decisions regarding the educational paradigm and general strategy are made at the national level. The government that makes decisions on national or regional standards can support the introduction of ICT-based goals, targets, and standards in schools. Obviously, this cannot be done simultaneously and with the same depth in all schools.

However, the enthusiasm engendered among educators on receiving technology can be used to develop a vocal constituency for the broad introduction of technologies into the educational practice of these schools. Even in schools that are generally not enthusiastic and engaged in technology, a teacher or a student will be given a chance to become a catalyst for future change. Educational authorities can combine approaches in formulating content and methods for an ICT agenda within a school system, region, or country. These include:

Explicit formulation of new priorities and new models of learning in standards and objectives of education—a key factor in the process of introducing ICT. Some of these standards may refer directly to ICT while others may not. Inclusion of elements of the application of ICT into curriculum guidelines of different subjects. Introduction of courses on technology or ICT in which priority is given to new goals for education and applications of ICT in integrative projects with other subjects.

Educational authorities should provide quality software and educational support, which can be done on the basis of licensing for a region. Authorities can decide to concentrate support on a special project that is interesting to several schools, or on a system of projects.

Distance education (in and out of school) in elementary and secondary schools also needs human (teacher, parent) participation in close contact with the learner. Parents should recognise the need to build new levels of relationship with their children and should consider the computer as a vehicle for building, rather than an obstacle to, family cohesion, and, finally, the family's learning culture. In some cases, parents constitute an important force in support of ICT in school.

Clubs and community centres provide access to ICT for many young learners, especially in communities where an individual computer is a luxury. For socially disadvantaged children, who often are not involved in formal education, such clubs provide an opportunity to be integrated into society. Resource centres and qualified personnel who work at several schools in a locality can be effective at certain stages of introducing ICT into education.

One of the main functions of schools is to provide an environment in which students can design and construct any number of physical and virtual worlds with which to interact and accumulate direct learning experience. This learning by doing links the mind and body and facilitates knowing, remembering, and the practical implementation of what is learned. Any learning environment of the kind described immediately above must have varied connections to the world outside the classroom, including manipulative and construction kits that model the universe, society, and technology, observations of nature, and productive activities. These connections should extend to consulting with eminent scientists, engineers and artists, and inviting local political figures and entrepreneurs for roundtable talks, and to project planning with the students.

The richly connected school of the future can be described by using the Vygotskian metaphor of zone of proximal development. The zone of a school consists of areas in which the school (represented by its teachers and the whole learning environment) is ready and eager to move forward - in the case, in using ICT. The zone also reflects the position of the school in the community of other schools. For example, a school has an IT-teacher who is discussing with a science teacher an opportunity to implement an environmental project connected with information that appeared in a local TV-broadcast and newspapers. Determining the zone of proximal development is based on:

i) achieved results;

ii) technical skills of teachers and students;

iii) project activity of the chosen schools;

iv) individual planning of all aspects of new technology introduction, including hardware configuration, curriculum and timetable changes, administrative applications; and

v) development of communities of teachers and schools, including internet user groups, clubs, seminars, publications, connecting with international communities, sources of information, scientists and other people who can provide first-hand information for school activities.

For the purpose of money allocation (region or municipal), decision-makers can use the model of the zone of proximal development and collect proposals from schools and impose qualification requirements. The simplest requirement for receiving ICT equipment is for schools to have an ICT-based curriculum, specified teachers, and a two- to three-year plan for the use of ICT for a given fraction of all lessons. They may also plan other aspects such as sources of teacher support. In this case, competition among schools usually turns out to be minimal. This procedure should be supported by follow-up plans.

9.1. Impact of ICT on Teaching and Learning

With widespread use of information and communication technologies (ICT), there is understandable interest in the impact of ICT on teaching and learning. Computer technologies and the internet have the potential to change both teaching and learning. Schools and classrooms are being equipped without adequate research or attention to the professional preparation of teachers. The belief that classrooms should be equipped with technology is predicated on the belief that technology can improve the rate, quality, amount, and effectiveness of learning

Many studies show that preschoolers are "learning optimists" who rate their own abilities highly, underestimate task difficulty, and hold positive expectations of success. During middle childhood, children begin to distinguish ability, effort, and external factors in explaining their performance. How they attribute success and failure on tasks influences the likelihood of developing an intrinsic motivation to persist at challenging tasks and the development of effective metacognitive skills. This in turn influences performance on academic tasks.

Research supports conventional wisdom indicating that students who are positively disposed toward tasks or subject matter are likely to learn more and learn more easily. For this reason, student attitudes toward computer use could have an impact on their learning. Academic achievement does not improve simply as a result of having access to computers in the classroom. If students are being exposed to less qualified instruction, it is constructive to note that the addition of computerised tasks designed by capable instructors has a positive effect on academic achievement. But it is misleading to portray the role of computers so positively while downplaying the importance of quality instruction.

There are many examples of innovative programmes combining access to technology with instruction designed to complement the new technological resources. Dramatic increases in reading and spelling performance of kindergarten students who were exposed to a computer-based reading and spelling programme over those not exposed to a computerised programme. In addition, one very well controlled study found a clear, positive relationship between the use of hypermedia instruction and achievement in engineering courses. There is thus some empirical support for a positive effect of technologies on student performance.

Children are not adults—their motor skills, cognitive abilities, and motivations are different. There are few studies on how computer systems and learning environments are designed, constructed, and maintained. The design of the learning environment also includes the ratio of computers-to-students, affecting the size of learning groups that can be formed. There was one computer to every nine elementary students, one to every eight lower secondary students, and one to every seven upper secondary students. The availability of computers does not appear to be a factor in educational outcomes under such conditions.

The nature of hardware and software affects both its use by and its impact on the learner. There is as yet very little comprehensive or rigorous research investigating the software design and the effects of design features on student learning and performance. The software programmes used in schools receive very poor evaluations, despite a clear understanding that instructional materials are more effective if their development has been informed by research.

Metacognitive knowledge includes knowledge about the self, the task, and strategies for learning. Memory and general problem solving skills also play a role in the effective use of metacognitive resources. The development and implementation of successful metacognitive skills can significantly influence learning and scholastic performance.

The peer-based interaction at the computer allows for exploration of the relationships between cognitive, metacognitive, and social processes. In particular, co-operative learning on computers is argued to facilitate peer interaction and have implications for motivation, self-esteem, and social behaviours. The extent of group effectiveness, at least in the 9-12 age group, is determined by several crucial factors, including the degree of autonomy developed by students, type of negotiation within a group, and the extent to which pupils appropriate the task

One of the major technological attempts to encourage the use of rehearsal strategies in learning, and thus better retention of information, has been the use of computer-assisted instruction (CAI). There is a general argument that using computers makes pupils better problem solvers and autonomous learners by encouraging the development of independent thinking skills beginning as young as preschool.

Instructional strategies vary in relation to the nature of the content and in relation to characteristics of the learner. For this reason, elementary students require more and more cognitive control over their artistic creativity as they develop, and thus programmes should be devised that allow them this control while at the same time encouraging their artistic expression.

9.2. Approaches to the Development of ICT in Secondary Education

Studies of ICT development in both developed and developing countries identify at least four broad approaches through which educational systems and individual schools proceed in their adoption and use of ICT. These four approaches, termed emerging, applying, infusing, and transforming, represent a continuum depicted as the model in Figure 9.1.

9.2.1. Emerging Approach

Schools at the beginning stages of ICT development demonstrate the emerging approach. Such schools begin to purchase, or have had donated, some computing equipment and software. In this initial phase, administrators and teachers are just starting to explore the possibilities and consequences of using ICT for school management and adding ICT to the curriculum. Schools at this emerging phase are still firmly grounded in traditional, teacher-centred practice. The curriculum reflects an increase in basic skills but there is an awareness of the uses of ICT.

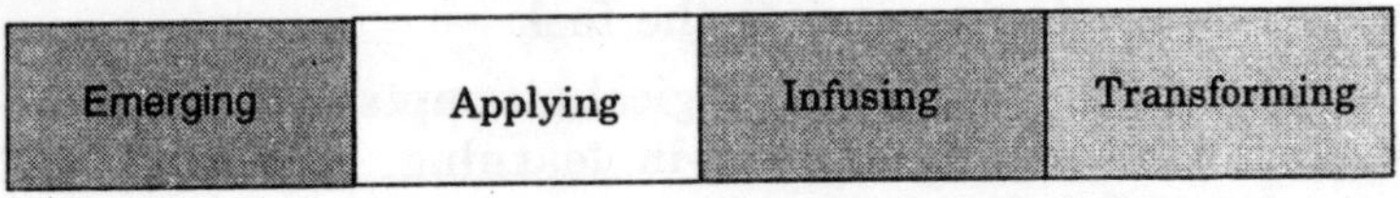

Figure 9.1. Model depicting a continuum of approaches to ICT development in schools

The emerging approach is linked with schools at the beginning stages of ICT development. Such schools begin to purchase computer equipment and software or perhaps have had some donated. In this initial phase, administrators and teachers are just starting to explore the possibilities and consequences of adding ICT for school management and the curriculum. The school is still firmly grounded in traditional, teacher-centred practice. For example, teachers tend to lecture and provide content while students listen, take notes, and are assessed on the prescribed content. School organisation provides discrete time periods for each subject. Learners' access to technology is through individual teachers.

In the emerging approach to ICT development, the focus is on the technical functions and uses of ICT and on the need for some knowledge and representation of the impacts of ICT systems as a whole. This approach often involves teachers' personal use of ICT, such as, for instance, the use of word processing to prepare worksheets, locating information on CD-ROMs or on the internet, or communicating with friends and family by email. Here, teachers are developing their ICT literacy and learning how to apply ICT to a range of personal and professional tasks. The emphasis is on training in a range of tools and applications, and increasing teachers' awareness of the opportunities for applying ICT to their teaching in the future.

9.2.2. Applying Approach

The applying approach is linked with schools in which a new understanding of the contribution of ICT to learning has developed. In this phase, administrators and teachers use ICT for tasks already carried out in school management and in the curriculum. Teachers still largely dominate the learning environment. For example, instructing may be supplemented with ICT such as electronic slide presentations and word-processed handouts. Students receive instruction and add notes to teacher prepared handouts. They use ICT tools to complete required lessons and are assessed on prescribed content.

School organisation provides discrete time periods for each subject with some flexibility to combine subjects and time periods. Learner access to technology is through one or two classroom computers and computer labs. Until now, ICT has been taught as a separate subject area. To move to the next phase, the school chooses to implement an ICT-based curriculum that increases ICT across various subject areas with the use of specific tools and software.

Those schools in which a new understanding of the contribution of ICT to learning has developed exemplify the applying approach. In this secondary phase, administrators and teachers use ICT for tasks already carried out in school management and in the curriculum. Teachers largely dominate the learning environment. Schools at the applying approach phase adapt the curriculum in order to increase the use of ICT in various subject areas with specific tools and software. This curriculum assists movement to the next approach if so desired.

In the applying approach, teachers use ICT for professional purposes, focusing on improving their subject teaching in order to enrich how they teach with a range of ICT applications. This approach often involves teachers in integrating ICT to teach specific subject skills and knowledge; beginning to change their methodology in the classroom; and using ICT to support their training and professional development. Teachers gain confidence in a number of generic and specialised ICT tools that can be applied to the teaching of their subject area. The opportunity to apply ICT in all their teaching is often limited only by a lack of ready access to ICT facilities and resources, which is why it is not fully integrated into all lessons for all students.

9.2.3. Infusing Approach

The infusing approach is linked with schools that now have a range of computer-based technologies in laboratories, classrooms, and administrative areas. Teachers explore new ways in which ICT changes their personal productivity and professional practice. The curriculum begins to merge subject areas to reflect real-world applications. For example, content is provided from multiple sources, including community and global resources through the world wide web. Students' access to technology enables them to choose projects and ICT tools that stimulate learning and demonstrate their knowledge across subject areas. School organisation provides the flexibility to combine subjects and time periods. Learners have more choices with regard to learning styles and pathways. They take more responsibility for their own learning and assessment.

At the next stage, the infusing approach involves integrating or embedding ICT across the curriculum, and is seen in those schools that now employ a range of computer-based technologies in laboratories, classrooms, and administrative offices. Teachers explore new ways in which ICT changes their personal productivity and professional practice. The curriculum begins to merge subject areas to reflect real-world applications.

9.2.3.1. Improving student learning and management

In the infusing approach to ICT development, ICT infuses all aspects of teachers' professional lives in such ways as to improve student learning and the management of learning processes. The approach supports active and creative teachers who are able to stimulate and manage the learning of students, integrating a range of preferred learning styles and uses of ICT in achieving their goals. The infusing approach often involves teachers easily integrating different knowledge and skills from other subjects into project-based curricula.

In this approach, teachers fully integrate ICT in all aspects of their professional lives to improve their own learning and the learning of their students. They use ICT to manage not only the learning of their students but also their own learning. They use ICT to assist all students to assess their own learning in achieving specific personal projects. In this approach, it becomes quite natural to collaborate with other teachers in solving common problems and to share their teaching experiences with others.

9.2.4. Transforming Approach

Schools that use ICT to rethink and renew school organisation in creative ways are at the transforming approach. ICT becomes an integral though invisible part of daily personal productivity and professional practice. The focus of the curriculum is now learner-centred and integrates subject areas in real-world applications. ICT is taught as a separate subject at the professional level and is incorporated into all vocational areas. Schools have become centres of learning for their communities.

Studies of teaching and learning in schools around the world identify four broad stages in the way that teachers and students learn about and gain confidence in the use of ICT. These four stages give rise to the model depicted in Figure 9.2 that shows the stages in terms of discovering, learning how, understanding how and when, and specialising in the use of ICT tools.

9.2.4.1. Transforming teaching through ICT

The transforming approach is linked with schools that have used ICT creatively to rethink and renew school organisation. ICT becomes an integral though invisible part of the daily personal productivity and professional practice. The focus of the curriculum is now much more learner-centred and integrates subject areas in real-world applications. For example, students may work with community leaders to solve local problems by accessing, analysing, reporting, and presenting information with ICT tools. Learners' access to technology is broad and unrestricted. They take even more responsibility for their own learning and assessment. ICT is taught as a subject area at an applied level and is incorporated into all vocational areas. The school has become a centre of learning for the community.

In the transforming approach to ICT development, teachers and other school staff regard ICT as so natural and part of the everyday life of schools that they begin to look at the process of teaching and learning in new ways. The emphasis changes from teacher-centred to learning-centred. Teachers, together with their students, expect a continuously changing teaching methodology designed to meet individual learning objectives.

Advances in technology and the way technology is incorporated into a system is a dynamic process. Each school must work within the context of its own system to fit choices to what best suits its unique situation and culture. Even within a school, various units or courses may use different approaches. The approaches are hierarchical with the emerging approach as a beginning point, and the transforming approach as a goal many perceive as the future of education.

9.3. Curriculum Design for Secondary Schools

The model depicted in Figure 9.2 is useful in developing the structure of a curriculum designed for both teachers and students to improve their knowledge and skills in ICT. The design supplies four curriculum areas tied to the four stages of teaching and learning, allowing schools to progress from:

i) ICT Literacy (where ICT skills are taught and learned as a separate subject) to

ii) Application of ICT in subject areas (where ICT skills are developed within separate subjects) to

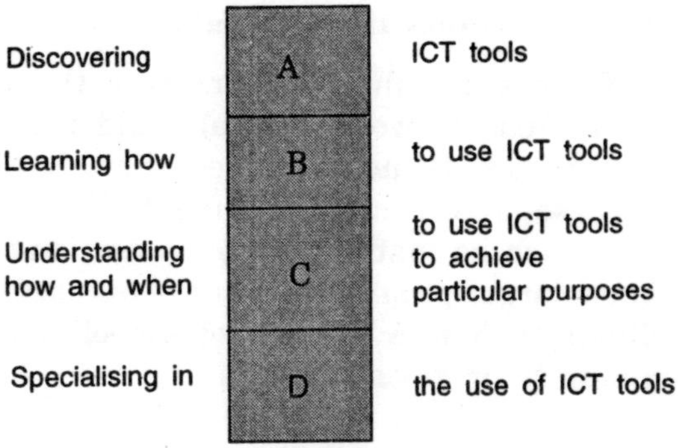

Figure 9.2. Model of stages of teaching and learning with and through ICT

iii) Infusing ICT across the curriculum (where ICT is integrated or embedded across all subjects of the curriculum) to

iv) ICT specialisation (where ICT is taught and learned as an applied subject or to prepare for a profession).

9.3.1. ICT Literacy

This curriculum area covers the use of ICT as encountered in the daily life of many communities. Specific units include basic concepts of ICT, using computers and managing files, word processing, spreadsheets, databases, creating presentations, finding information and communicating with computers, social and ethical issues, and jobs using ICT. The International Computer Driving Licence, which derived from the European Computer Driving Licence, was helpful in the organisation of this area of the curriculum.

9.3.2. Application of ICT Tools

This area of the curriculum covers the application of ICT tools for working within specific subject areas such as languages, natural sciences, mathematics, social sciences, and art. Specific units include measurement, modelling and simulation, robots and feedback devices, statistics, creating graphics, spreadsheet design, and database design.

9.3.3. Infusing ICT across the curriculum

This area of the curriculum demonstrate the use of ICT across subject areas to work on real-world projects and to solve real problems. Some examples show how, within a particular course, ICT can help students integrate several subject areas, such as mathematics, science, and art. Other examples show larger projects that cut across several subject areas or illustrate how a number of schools can integrate ICT in community or global projects.

9.3.4. ICT specialisation

This area of the curriculum is designed for students who plan to go into professions that use ICT such as, for example, engineering, business, and computer science, or for students who plan to advance to higher education. Content covers the use of advanced tools and techniques for the ICT specialist. Specific units include basic and advancing programming, planning information systems, designing process control systems, and project management.

9.3.4.1. Discovering ICT tools

The first stage (Stage A in Figure 9.2) that teachers and learners go through in ICT development is of discovering ICT tools and their general functions and uses. In this discovery stage, there is usually an emphasis on ICT literacy and basic skills. This stage of discovering ICT tools is linked with the emerging approach in ICT development.

9.3.4.2. How to use ICT tools

Following on from the discovery of ICT tools comes the stage of learning how to use ICT tools, and beginning to make use of them in different disciplines (Stage B in Figure 9.2). This stage involves the use of general or particular applications of ICT, and is linked with the applying approach in ICT development.

9.3.4.3. Understanding how and when to use ICT tools

The next stage (Stage C in Figure 9.2) is understanding how and when to use ICT tools to achieve a particular purpose, such as in completing a given project. This stage implies the ability to recognise situations where ICT will be helpful, choosing the most appropriate tools for a particular task, and using these tools in combination to solve real problems. This stage is linked with the infusing and transforming approaches in ICT development.

9.3.4.4. Specialising in the use of ICT tools

The fourth and last stage (Stage D in Figure 9.2) involves specialising in the use of ICT tools such as occurs when one enters more deeply into the science that creates and supports ICT. In this stage students study ICT as a subject to become specialists.

9.4. Characteristics of ICT Development

There are various characteristics of schools, or aspects of school leadership, that relate to a school's progress in ICT development. These characteristics of schools that have an effect on ICT development within schools.

9.4.1. Vision

Vision refers to the aspirations and goals of both individuals within a school and the school system as a whole. As the school advances, the mission statements should become clearer and provide a basis for decisionmaking. Mission statements should help individual members of the learning community visualise a school's aspirations for the future and act in harmony.

9.4.2. Philosophy of Learning and Pedagogy

Ways in which teachers and students interact and how the school is managed for learning are part of what is meant by a school's philosophy of learning and pedagogy. These philosophies will necessarily characterise the ways in which

ICT is incorporated into a school. A setting that is dominated by the teacher as the main provider of subject content is adopting a teacher-centred philosophy. The teacher controls the use of ICT in such a setting as well. A learnercentred philosophy, by contrast, describes a setting where content comes from a variety of resources, and where projects are chosen and designed by the students. ICT tools and resources are selected by students in ways that match the aims of a project best. These contrasting approaches to pedagogy are sometimes referred to as instructivist and constructivist respectively.

9.4.3. Development Plans and Policies

How a school's vision and teaching philosophies are carried out is translated into development plans and policies. In the detailed steps of such plans and policies, goals and objectives are further defined providing interim and long-term targets. Policies are set, a budget is allocated, facilities are determined, roles are defined, tasks are delegated, and an evaluation plan is created to define the direction ICT development will take.

9.4.4. Facilities and Resources

The learning environment in which ICT is used requires certain facilities and resources. Facilities include basic infrastructure such as electrical wiring, internet access, lighting, air-conditioning, and space. Decisions on inclusion or lack of ergonomic design and choice of furniture impact not only on use of ICT, but also on the health and well being of users. Resources include various types of technological devices from computers with peripherals, video equipment, and specialised tools like digital microscopes. Further resources include various types of software, as well as traditional tools like books, videos, and audiotapes.

9.4.5. Understanding the Curriculum

An understanding of the curriculum affects the progression of ICT in the curriculum in following various stages of development. First, is an awareness stage in which students become ICT literate with regard to what technology is available and how it might be used. Second, as students learn basic skills, they begin to apply various ICT tools to their regular learning assignments and projects. Third, as students become more capable and confident with ICT, they begin to integrate and overlap both subject areas and tools. Last, is the applied use of ICT in which students are now enabled to address larger, more complex, real-world professional issues.

9.4.6. Professional Development of School Staff

In parallel with the curriculum for students, there must be professional development of the staff within a school. The personal productivity and professional practice of teachers are enhanced with the use of ICT. First, is an awareness stage in which teachers and staff become ICT literate with regard to what technology is available and how it might be used. Second, as teachers and staff learn basic skills, they begin to apply various ICT tools to their regular tasks and projects. Third, as teachers and staff become more capable and confident with ICT, they begin to integrate and overlap both subject areas and tools. Last, is a change in professional practice in which teachers are now enabled to design lessons to incorporate larger, more complex, real-world projects using ICT tools and resources.

As ICT is introduced into school systems, there is a tendency to move from discrete skills training to reflective practice and integrative professional development. Budgetary allocation and provision for release time for teacher professional development seriously impact on the ability of a school system to incorporate ICT in a meaningful way.

9.4.7. Community Involvement

Community involvement may include parents, families, businesses, industry, government agencies, private foundations, social, religious and professional organisations, as well as other educational institutions such as vocational schools and universities. Community involvement can come in the form of donations of equipment and resources, or may be in human resources provided for training and technical assistance. As a community contributes to a school, so the school can give back in many ways. For example, a school may decide to provide community members with evening access to computer labs, or have students offer training to parents. The use of ICT provides an opportunity for a school and its students to interact with both local and global communities. Interaction may range from building websites for community organisations, to sharing projects with remote schools.

9.5. Effective Designs for Educators

Emerging new technologies can be powerful allies in efforts to improve teaching and learning. For technologies to play a truly comprehensive role in reshaping the nature of schooling, however, they must support a broader vision of educational change. Technologies that are well designed and well integrated into instruction can help bring about and sustain these kinds of changes in our classrooms. Communications technologies provide teachers and students with opportunities to share, discuss, and exchange ideas with larger communities of learners.

Simulations, microworlds, and other discovery-oriented programs create environments in which students can apply thinking skills to solve real-world problems, students can work readily together in groups, and teachers—freed from certain classroom management tasks—can become guides and coaches to students. Software composition tools, such as word processors, scanners, desktop publishing programs, and video cameras, enable students to express what they know in the form of tangible products, and these products in turn can stimulate further conversation and learning and offer new forms of assessment. Digital storage media, with their great capacity and flexibility, allow teachers and students to pursue a wide range of inquiries into complex subject matter that are tailored to individual interests and needs, and this can motivate students to learn more.

9.5.1. Digital Archives

Archival institutions are among the most exciting resources driving educational interest in information-based, multimedia technologies. Collections are being digitised, providing classroom teachers with access to artifacts and information previously available only to specialised scholars or academic researchers. The presence of these collections on the world wide web gives teachers and students opportunities to work with an extraordinary array of authentic materials and up-to-date information. It is precisely the depth, scope, and multiple media nature of such collections that makes them particularly challenging to structure and present in ways that are truly useful to educators and their students.

Too often, the developers of various online educational resources have neglected the particular interests of and significant constraints faced by educators. The creation of digital libraries and archives provides an opportunity to address the design concerns of teachers and students in a challenging but highly rewarding context. The first international research conference on the theory and practice of creating digital libraries was held in June 1994, and a second was held in June 1995. More than 60 papers were presented at these meetings, representing diverse organisations from around the world. One such paper, written by collaborators on the University of Michigan's Digital Library Project, notes that the growth of information archives has the potential to achieve the following goals:

i) Provide information at any time and in any place;
ii) Provide access to collections of multimedia information that integrate text, image, graphics, audio, video, and other continuous media;
iii) Make it possible for users to personalise or customise how they access and represent information for example, by "harvesting" only relevant information and avoiding information overload; and

iv) Radically enhance collaborative intellectual activities, including research, learning, and design, by reducing barriers of geography, organisational distance, and time.

In addition to practical problems of access, classroom teachers face a number of obstacles in using and interpreting information-rich resources, and making them relevant to their students. Teachers have different purposes and initially bring different training to the job. There is abundant evidence demonstrating that access and training are key factors that consistently complicate efforts to integrate technology into the classroom.

Gaining access to technology resources—particularly the high-speed network connections required to connect to the world wide web—is often the first hurdle that schools must overcome. Limited finances and lack of community awareness can make this a significant hurdle for school districts. It is also well documented that the ongoing training of teachers in how to integrate technology resources in the curriculum is just as important as basic access. While these issues continue to be chronic challenges for technology integration efforts, two related problems are particularly relevant to thinking about the design of online resources for educators: teacher time and limited contexts or incentives for intellectual exploration.

The nature of schooling is such that most teachers are required to teach a curriculum that they played little or no role in designing and have only limited opportunities to adapt. Our educational system tends to foster a form of intellectual disempowerment in which K-12 teachers are commonly viewed as implementers of state- and district-mandated curricula rather than shapers and interpreters of powerful ideas and methodologies. Often teacher education is built on these assumptions as well. These constraints are brought to the fore when teachers begin to work with the kinds of resources that academic scholars and scientists use. It is the job of scholars and scientists to make new knowledge based on their engagement with these resources.

And yet, our education system commonly limits teachers from engaging in precisely this kind of work.

If digital archives are to be of genuine value to elementary and secondary educators and their students, we must think differently and creatively about how best to support them in making substantive and relevant use of these resources. The following three key design considerations are make large digital archives accessible and engaging in schools:

i) teacher ownership,

ii) student engagement, and

iii) education-relevant search engines.

9.5.2. Teacher Ownership

Developers of print and multimedia educational materials often assume that for their products to be used productively in classrooms, they must be made "teacher proof"—designed in a way that leaves little or no room for experimentation or invention by teachers and students. For example, teachers' guides, rather than creating opportunities for interpretation and ownership, often contain lockstep approaches to teaching and learning. This approach is being challenged widely by educators and researchers who advocate classrooms based on active, constructive teaching and learning processes: solving problems, communicating, reasoning, exploring, inventing, and proving.

Increasingly, professional teaching associations and groups involved in education reform are seeking to articulate standards for students that emphasise thinking over memorisation. Although these efforts have gone a long way toward reshaping our understanding of the classroom teacher's roles and responsibilities, the publishing industry is still heavily dominated by a mindset that discourages inventiveness in teachers and students.

The decentralised architecture of the internet offers opportunities to build resources for teachers that are not governed by the preconceptions of educational publishers. The world wide web has the potential to serve as an alternative forum, in which developers and designers can experiment with formats that enable educators to bring archival resources into their curricula in ways that make sense to them. We have found that ownership—the process of generating ideas and strategies that make sense within the particular circumstances of one's own classroom and curriculum—is a key to successful use of digital archives. One possible design approach is to provide teachers with an analytical tool kit that can support different kinds of analyses of resource materials.

Analytic tools—such as story boards, spreadsheets, image analysis tools, databases, timelines, templates that describe the content and structure of documents, and resource tools that enable teachers to construct relevant content links—could help teachers evaluate and assemble their own information resources. For example, if teachers and students are studying the history of the civil rights movement and have access to a digital archive containing photographs of key historical events associated with this period, they can use a timeline tool to construct their own understandings of the narrative events that define the era.

Rather than building lesson plans that tell teachers how and when to use archival materials, designers of digital educational resources could develop activity templates that illustrate potential uses of their tools, and could make them available through the world wide web. In some cases, as with story boards or image analysis tools, the templates would be the tools themselves. In other cases, the templates would illustrate ways to use archival materials with off-the-shelf spreadsheets, databases, and timelines.

Online conversation spaces would be a key component this tool-based approach. Here teachers could generate and share ideas online about how to use analytic tools with different types of information archives. Discussion groups, organised by topic, grade level, and approach (for example, scientific analysis, visual literacy, or historical understanding) would be an essential part of these online resources.

9.5.3. Student Engagement

In the elementary grades, a student's sense of self is very important, and students develop better understanding in all disciplines when they can connect the subject of study to their own lives. In elementary social studies, for example, teachers might use photographs, diaries, and other historical artifacts to encourage students to compare what life was like at a particular time in the past with life nowadays. Students might also use timelines, maps, and other visual aids to put past events in chronological order, draw connections among them, and make sense of a sea of information.

Designers and teachers might also highlight themes that younger children are passionate about such as "How do animals protect themselves?" to guide student forays into biological databases or archives. Designers of resources for the elementary level can make concepts that often seem abstract and remote more familiar and accessible by building in creative ways for children to look and investigate.

Middle school students require a different approach to teaching and learning. Students at this age enjoy inquiries and arguments, and archival materials can become evidence for solving a larger intellectual quest or puzzle. Middle school students relish problems of interpretation; by piecing together information from a number of different documents or artifacts, they can begin to develop a better understanding of the meaning of each source and can draw conclusions based on the evidence.

In the humanities, for example, historical narratives, documents, photographs, oral histories, and art can be used to build hypotheses about the historical context in which the sources were created. One compelling way to use archival materials with this age group is to construct a mystery that students answer by hunting for and piecing together clues contained in or across digital archives; this kind of information hunt can be part of a larger inquiry.

At the high school level, students are capable of sophisticated inquiry; they also need to feel passionate about and connected to the issues they are studying. Building connections between the subject area being studied and the issues of real concern to high school students is of paramount importance. Issues of fairness, leadership, and responsibility are examples of themes that can stimulate students to engage with archival materials.

For example, students can use scientific databases as core resources for local environmental projects. Or they can use archives that contain historical advertisements to compare past representations of women with their contemporary portrayals. In sum, to make digital archives accessible, designers must carefully consider the developmentally relevant cognitive and affective characteristics of students at different ages. The best informants for developers are likely to be the students and teachers themselves.

9.5.4. Education-Relevant Search Engines

One of the most complex tasks associated with using archival materials effectively is the ability to search and browse through large quantities of information in a way that makes conceptual and logistical sense. Indexing schemes that work well for a classroom teacher are likely to be very different from those that function effectively for a scientist or scholar. Many of the indexing schemes currently used by digital libraries and other archival institutions are based on a standard bibliographic categorisation system (the same one that exists on the bottom of library index cards).

Institutions that digitise material find this to be the most efficient way of referencing materials while preserving traditional categorising system familiar to researchers, scholars, and archivists. But this system was developed during an era when people had to come to libraries, and materials had to be physically organised on shelves. The digital world redefines the concept of categorisation and offers new possibilities. To make the best use of the more extensive and flexible digital resources, teachers and students need to be able to build their own approaches to cataloguing archival materials.

References

Alspaugh, J. W., "The relationship between number of students per computer and educational outcomes", *Journal of Educational Computing Research*, *21*, 141-150, 1999.

Baron, L., D'Amico, M., Sissons, M., & Peters, P., "Attributions, group size and exposure time as predictors, of elementary children's performance on a microcomputer task", *Computers in Human Behavior*, *12*, 145-157, 1996.

Borton, W., "The effects of computer managed mastery learning on mathematics test scores in the elementary school", *Journal of Computer Based Instruction*, *15*, 95-98, 1989.

Bracewell. R., Laferrière, T., Breuleux, A., Benoit, J., & Abdous, M., *The emerging contribution of online resources and tools to classroom learning and teaching*, Ottawa, Rescol Canada, 1998.

Coley, R., Cradler, J., & Engel, P., *Computers and Classrooms: The Status of Technology in US schools*, Princeton, NJ: Policy Information Center, Educational Testing Sevice, 1997.

10

Teachers' and Administrators' Approach to Curriculum

An important role of ICT inside a school is that of providing a new framework that can foster a revision and an improvement of teaching and learning practices. Though many positive results have been reported on a small scale, there has been no breakthrough in learning improvements because of ICT on a large, replicable scale. Nevertheless, teachers and students can take advantage of the growing availability of educational resources as software packages and Web pages.

Teachers will need curricula-related content and clear strategies and examples to effectively use these materials in the classroom. They will find that students can become highly motivated towards learning (and even toward regularly attending school) if technology makes up part of their classroom experience. Teachers can fruitfully use this positive attitude to explore new learning strategies in which students can be more actively involved in learning, as opposed to being simply passive information receivers. Collaborative, project-based and self-paced learning are just a few alternatives amply documented and particularly appropriate to use when ICT are present.

Primary and secondary students with special talents (i.e. mathematics, music or literature) will find a vast amount of digital tools and resources as well as groups of similarly inclined youngsters all over the world with whom to share and develop their talents. On the other hand, students with special needs will also find resources and tools for remedial or self-paced learning. This can have a particularly high impact on more deprived and culturally isolated schools where primary students have fewer information resources and learning opportunities.

However, it is important to emphasise that it is not the presence of technology in itself (or of outstanding and guaranteed learning software, if such thing exists) that will stimulate significant changes inside a school. Without teacher involvement, most students in primary levels in particular, but also in higher levels may not take advantage of all the available potential on their own. Teachers need to become active participants for effective ICT educational use, such as providing guidance, help and usage rules for the students. Teachers are needed to organise the learning spaces and to guide toward the achievement of significant learning objectives.

In developing countries, students often do not acquire sufficient mathematical skills, a basic understanding of scientific concepts or an adequate reading comprehension level during their school years. ICT provides tools and content to exe rcise these abilities, which will be needed to take advantage of the vast amount of content present in today's networks. Information processing skills to transform data (i.e. searching, selecting, synthesising and communicating information) into knowledge is rapidly becoming a basic requirement for the emergent information society.

If ICT policies are closely related to the curriculum, teachers will more likely use them for learning practices in classrooms. Therefore, curriculum designers should consider the inclusion of ICT as transversal themes, i.e. in all curricular sectors, and in the curriculum-specification guidelines that will be used by teachers. It is not advisable to have ICT as separate, isolated technical subjects or sectors in the curriculum (e.g. programming, software tools and hardware configurations), because in this atmosphere, teachers will tend to regard ICT as special subjects and may not integrate them in their normal practice.

10.1. Cultural, Social, and Professional Roles of ICT

The cultural, social and professional roles of ICT are exercised primarily through an effective use of the vast amount of information sources and services available today via Internet and CD-based content for the entire educational community: students, teachers, administrators and parents. Also, nowadays new equipment and low-cost portable keyboards5 with text -handling capacities are helping teachers around the world with their professional routines.

A school connected to the Internet can foster communication at local (i.e. inside a community), national and international levels. Educational projects that connect students and teachers from different countries might amplify the quality of the conversational spaces, may expand students' horizons by allowing them to know and interact with people from other cultures and can stimulate group work and social interaction.

For teachers, networks provide a medium to establish fluent links among peers from schools worldwide. Teachers can benefit greatly from sharing their experiences, problems and queries with colleagues in same situations. Of similar importance is the growing field of e-learning, with the availability of a large number of training courses for teachers delivered through the Internet, thus providing new means for professional development regardless of the teacher's workplace.

A low bandwidth and/or poor quality communication infrastructure can restrict network usability to text -only e-mails, limited to a few times a week. This is a far cry from the potential benefits of e-learning and from participating in professional groups and learning circles using high bandwidth connections. This is particularly important for geographically and/or culturally isolated schools, which are common in rural and suburban areas. With up-to-date communications technology in place, students and teachers in these settings may experience a reduction in their cultural isolation and a significant improvement in their learning resources. Again, this will be highly dependent on the quality of the telecommunications infrastructure and its cost.

10.1.1. Administrative Roles

ICT have important roles to play in making school administration less burdensome and more effectively integrated to the official information flow about students, curricula, teachers, budgets and activities through the educational system information pipelines. They are also a good means for informing community members (parents, politicians, and researchers) about educational news and policies.

At the classroom level, teachers can more easily keep student's marks and their personal and academic records permanently up-to-date, as well as produce all required data for school administration and for parents, using preformatted documents. Most importantly, teachers can maintain their subject content (lesson plans, exercises, evaluation) in digital format, making it easy to update, to share with other teachers and to enhance with time. In fact, the many ways tools such as a computer, a handheld device or a portable keyboard (and a network) can help a teacher in administrative tasks is one of the more convincing arguments to make to inexperienced teachers so they will accept training eagerly.

This should be carefully considered during teacher-training planning because before pedagogical use in the classroom, many teachers may prefer to become familiarised first with the technology outside the classroom. This can often be facilitated greatly by starting out with software applications or simple devices such as portable keyboards or handhelds that can be of immediate use. It is relatively easy to learn how to use these machines to store text in a portable keyboard, to construct spreadsheets, or to make use of word processing to record students' marks and records.

At the school level, administrators will appreciate the use of spreadsheets, word processors, small databases and special accounting software to organise and store all relevant data. At the educational system level, policy-makers may consider the introduction of ICT at all three levels (classroom, school, system) as a great opportunity to acquire and to distribute information through the system and from the general public to the classroom teacher. A coordinated effort can achieve economies of scale and compatibility of information processes and flows at all levels.

There are a number of software packages for all these levels of usage, which should be carefully evaluated by the teachers and the school administration to assess their completeness, their adaptability to the school's reality and the level of support offered by the software vendors.

10.1.2. Management Tools

Educational systems are known as stable institutions, not prone to rapid changes and innovations. It is possible that a significant number of teachers and school administrators will resist the introduction of ICT in their schools. At the most important level-the school-the pressure to provide and receive information to and from the central system digitally is a powerful message and a driving force towards change.

Centralised systems normally have a well-consolidated circuit of information flow to and from all levels of the system. A change in a general rule or ordinance generally moves gradually through the circuit until it eventually reaches the classroom teacher or the parents if it is relevant to them. It is an administrator's responsibility at each level to decide when to move each piece of information and to whom. This reflects a power structure that imposes restrictions on the transparent and rapid flow of information. ICT can have a rapid and powerful impact on this structure by changing the rules of information flow. For example, all educational information can be placed for the teachers, administrators, parents and the community at large on a public web site.

In the classroom, that human is the teacher, who controls the nature of the environment and what happens there. Good classroom tools extend the teacher's power to create a rich learning environment. If the teacher does not know what to make of the tool, or fears it, or misconstrues its uses, it will be used badly or not at all.

Staff development should be at the core of any policy for introducing ICT in education. Teachers are the key players in any educational innovation and the importance of considering their skills as well as their beliefs during training. It then reflects on the school as a workplace.

Moreover, ICTs at schools will have little impact if teachers are not actively involved in all phases of their integration to the curriculum. In other words, a major obstacle to an adequate use of technology across all grade levels and in the curriculum, is the lack of a critical mass of teachers who feel comfortable in using the technology and can provide support and exemplary instances of good practice to those who are still not fluent with technology.

Field researchers have learned that teachers work under a given social and cultural context that is a key influence in the way they perceive and use ICT for their personal and professional practices. A number of other factors that might affect teachers' decision to use ICT in the classroom. These factors can be grouped into the following two levels of barriers:

i) The "first order barriers" comprise a number of aspects that are extrinsic to teachers: access to technology, time for practice, technical support, resources and content, and training. Even if all these barriers were removed, most teachers would not automatically use technology.

ii) The "second order barriers" are intrinsic to teachers: attitudes, beliefs, practices and resistance. Teacher beliefs mediate their planning and classroom practices, in particular the belief about their level of ability to use ICT in classrooms. Self-efficacy, the belief about one's capability to perform actions at a given level, is based on the level of skill possessed and on judgments about what can be done with current skills.

A broad but useful generalisation about teachers' attitudes towards ICT is that of considering three basic categories of teachers: innovators, resistant and mainstream. Innovators will rapidly recognise the potential of ICT in education, will be willing to explore its uses with their students and in their professional duties (i.e. management) in the early stages of the training process. They will also be willing to become responsible for administrative and technical tasks related to the equipment.

Many good teachers are resistant to ICT with good and strong reasons that must be taken into account. Although many of them may never get actively involved in using computers in a lab, they will undoubtedly provide a healthy and necessary tension that will impose on policy-makers the need to use rigorous arguments in favor of ICT in schools. Also, these teachers can play a critical role against wholesale promises of improvements in education due to the introduction of computers and the Internet. Some of them may become active in resisting change, and because ICT programmes are bound to have failures sooner or later at many levels (i.e., poor hardware maintenance, incomp etent teacher trainers, etc.), and more so at larger scales, these failures will provide good ammunition for these teachers.

Some of these teachers' arguments against using ICT in education are that these technologies represent a threat to their professional status because they will diminish their role (i.e. stories about software that might substitute for them), will degrade their relationship with students and will take over initiative and control within the classroom to the detriment of teachers. Other teachers are simply not willing to make changes in their teaching praxis because they perceive it adequate as it is; still others are simply afraid of using computers and similar technologies such as TV recorders, cameras and screen projectors.

However, a teacher might carry a resistant attitude mainly because of a low level of confidence in his or her abilities. Success stories from other teachers might not be helpful to one with a low confidence level. Rather, simple administrative applications and off-classroom uses might be a good way to start with them. For example, keeping student's marks in a spreadsheet or sending e-mail to friends and relatives are easy-to-learn exercises that provide immediate reward that may strengthen self-confidence.

Mainstream teachers are late adopters of technology and are arguably the largest group and therefore the most important in the long run. Normally, if innovators provide them with good working examples and they see a clear path for their own familiarisation with the technology, as well as some incentives for their professional development, they will be more willing to give it a try.

Mainstream teachers with some confidence and with some level of skills can greatly benefit from a set of exemplary practices (in CD Rom or TV format), supplemented by lecture guides with an explicit and carefully designed instructions for ICT use in the classroom on each subject field. Besides the intrinsic complexity of hardware and software, teachers' pedagogical beliefs and their perceived confidence in using ICT in the classroom are critical aspects that must be considered in a staff development policy, particularly for mainstream and resistant teachers.

10.2. The ICT Coordinator

The ICT Coordinator is a teacher with special ICT training who has a central role in the school's long-term use of the technology. Some of the functions of the ICT Coordinator include the following:

i) *Technology*: To practice basic preventive maintenance of equipment (cleaning, inventory checks); hardware, network and software configuration. School interface with local or national hardware and software providers. Selecting and purchasing hardware and operating system upgrades. Administrative and educational software; maintaining virus protection and Internet content filters, according to teachers' needs.

ii) *Pedagogy*: To coordinate computer lab and software uses according to teachers' needs. Assisting teachertraining processes, facilitating and preparing resources and supplies and also performing training.

Helping to identify new uses of ICT inside the school and assisting teachers in implementing them.

iii) *Administrative*: To deal with school priorities and investments and negotiating the ICT budget with the school administrators.

However, support for ICT use on subjectspecific content teaching is more complex, and it requires a deeper involvement from the subject teacher. Coordinators can help in looking up web sites or searching for subject-related software in the market. However, pedagogical decisions about how and when to use a particular software or web site for learning purposes are more suitably in the hands of the subject teachers and the curriculum experts in each school.

Usually, only after a number of negotiations and with evidence of equipment failure and low usability rates, will school administrators start spending on an ICT Coordinator. A teacher with a similar training experience as the trainees can be very convincing by using more realistic examples and by being more in tune with classroom culture. Besides their role in training and guiding teachers towards pedagogical uses of ICT, trainers are permanently in close contact with both teachers and programme managers; therefore they also perform a few very important complementary roles:

i) Trainers become the ambassadors of the programme at the school, conveying information from programme headquarters to each teacher in the school. In this respect, trainers should be well-prepared to address a variety of questions in the school, from the technical to the pedagogical.

ii) Trainers provide feedback information to programme management in many fashions. They can gather useful data about the schools' training progress and difficulties. This can help to refine staff development activities in each geographical zone.

iii) Trainers can help organise an annual fair for all schools from a community or province. They have a number of goals. These include showing to parents, educational authorities and the community how the schools have progressed with ICT and demonstrating to other teachers what can be achieved with ICT in classrooms.

Some of the activities produced for trainers are the following:

i) Maintaining a special teacher-trainer's web site with an up-to-date record from each, with news from the programme, training documents, chat rooms and help desk. This site is the basis for gradually building up a community of trainers organised around subject matter and/or workplace (i.e. rural, vocational, religious school, etc.).

ii) Sending regular, personalised messages to trainers, with news about the programme in general and about the programme in the specific geographical school-zone of their responsibility.

iii) Providing trainers with copies of educational software and manuals to be distributed to the schools in their geographical school-zone.

iv) Organising at least twice a year face-to-face meetings of teacher-trainers, including educational authorities, so trainers can share their achievements, discuss their problems, anticipate future challenges, and request and coordinate their support.

It is often the case that teachers use ICT in classrooms in inadequate forms, basically "doing the same thing, but this time with technology." The opportunities to adapt more engaging and meaningful learning approaches are precisely what teachers should develop in classrooms. Therefore, a necessary (but still rather idealistic) requirement for teacher-trainers is that they know well the potential of ICT for fostering new learning environments and use appropriate state-of- the-art methodologies and software, such as project-based learning, learning by doing, and simulation software.

Through Internet, teachers are stimulated to participate in communities of learners from other schools (and even other countries) that share similar realities. Unfortunately, few teachers-mostly innovators-will pursue these initiatives after the training period, a situation which is under debate because of the constant energy required to get mainstream teachers to participate.

Many institutions (mostly universities but increasingly businesses as well) are offering web-based courses to train people for a variety of jobs. The web also contains courses intended for primary and secondary students, gradually increasing in number though still mostly in English. This trend is gaining momentum and in the near future, there will be probably a whole curriculum that students will be able to follow at their own pace and convenience, with mature content in many languages.

The benefits of e-learning and the opportunity to greatly improve students' learning by designing realistic simulations that can offer engaging learning-by-doing environments, for two reasons:

i) They can provide a cost-effective and efficient means to train teachers on ICT in a nationwide programme.

ii) They may positively enhance present classroom situations in which students are not motivated towards learning.

Therefore, each school offers a different kind and degree of acceptance of innovations such as the use of ICT in the curriculum. The school is a good place for teachers to learn how to integrate ICT in their praxis and to explore new ways of teaching; it is their workplace and an environment they share with students. Therefore, their own classroom might be the best place for training sessions, simulating a real setting with other teachers playing student roles or practicing with actual students.

A fundamental requirement for a successful staff development strategy is that teachers have time for hands-on practice with ICT during normal working hours. The introduction of ICT imposes some changes in the managing practices of schools. Different activities must be scheduled; additional bills must be paid, etc. It is therefore important that the management (leadership) of the school becomes involved in the training programme, ideally, on equal terms as everyone else.

This has positive impact in the near future and in the long-term future. First, by gaining familiarity with the use of ICT tools, managers will be more able to understand the needs and concerns of teachers. Second, it will allow the leadership to represent in more precise and realistic terms the school's achievements and its needs to other critical agents from the community, be they parents, educational authorities, or fellow educators. Finally, it will help them to better decide on matters of planning, budgeting and investing for the future development of the school.

10.2.1. Technology Acquisition

Undoubtedly, the most visible and media attractive side of an ICT Programme is children using computers in a classroom. However there is much more to an ICT Programme than deploying computers in the school system. The strong communicative power of this image, as compared to the lower visibility of training sessions with teachers, has often been one of the causes that technology is regarded as an end in itself, and for political decisionmakers to spend disproportionately more money on hardware than on teacher training.

Hardware is certainly a fundamental necessity in an ICT programme, but its effectiveness, and hence its return on investment, is probably proportional to the quality and effectiveness of the teacher-training programme. The decision of how much technology to purchase for each school and where to put it follows no fixed or standard set of rules applicable in every case. It is often the case that budgetary restrictions impose a single solution for every school, i.e. a fixed number of computers and a few printers clustered in a special room. This solution is often far from optimal, and several other factors should be taken into account.

Buying technology for schools can be a centralised or a decentralised process or a mixture of both. One benefit of making all technology acquisitions at a higher-than-school level is that the larger the number of devices, and therefore the amount of money involved, the more possible it is to obtain lower prices, better support services and often, less expensive software licenses. However, although this approach is often preferred because of the cost reduction, a one-size-fits-all solution will rarely be optimal for any one school.

In the long run, school administrators together with teachers and parents should be responsible for the decisions about what and how much technology to purchase for their school and proceed according to their specific needs. This will require them (i) to know precisely what technology is needed for their educational projects; (ii) to be well informed about the options and benefits of each piece of hardware and software available on the market; and (iii) to be capable of freely and directly negotiating with vendors to make the most out of their budget.

An intermediate approach between the full flexibility obtained when each school is buying on its own and the possible lower costs derived from the whole system's large scale buying strategy, is that of defining a set of characteristics that would fit 3-5 different school categories (i.e. school size, students per classroom, etc.) and purchasing a separate pre-defined configuration of hardware, software and services for each category.

Several other factors besides the number of devices should be considered when planning for technology implementation in schools. Among these, the most important ones are:

i) Maintenance

ii) Recurrent costs

iii) Electrical power system

iv) Furniture

v) Local area network.

vi) Security and access (i.e. for parents and other community members)

vii) Environmental conditions

Policy-makers should be aware of the rapid obsolescence of hardware and of the pressure from hardware vendors to replace equipment. Technology becomes obsolete only if it cannot be used properly for a given task. Computers, PDAs, portable keyboards and many other devices may last for more than a decade assisting with many useful tasks in a school, such as word processing and basic information storing and retrieving services. For example, many of these uses will require a computer with less than a 1GHz processor and with basic graphic capabilities (even as backup servers). It is also important to be aware that centrally performed hardware and software procurement procedures can take many months. This length of time is due to the many steps involved in a well-run procurement process:

a) The careful definition of the protocols (a rigorous design of the procurement forms and of the technical specifications may save time and avoid problems with vendors for whom the procurement, because of its relative large size, can be of strategic importance for their business);

b) The time allowed for the hardware and software vendors to analyse the procurement documents and to prepare their offers;

c) The time to revise and analyse each offer by the ICT policy implementation team (which probably should hire independent consultants for assistance and for reasons of transparency), and finally;

d) The time to deliver and deploy the goods in the schools.

There are basically three ICT deployment approaches that have been tried out in schools around the world, and all have advantages and some problems. One approach is the concentration of technology in specially networked rooms, known as "Technology Labs." Another is a decentralised system in which a number of devices are put inside each or most classrooms, the library and science labs. A third approach is a mixture of the previous two.

The centralised Technology Lab is the easier and less expensive plan to implement, but also less effective in terms of teacher involvement. It is less expensive because it is possible to define a limited number of standard room configurations, including computers, peripherals, local area networks, Internet connections, cabling, heating, safety, power, and furn iture that can be replicated in many similar schools and therefore acquired with economies of scale.

From a school perspective, concentrating all ICT resources in one special place for all possible uses (learning, teacher training and community involvement) makes its administration and maintenance easier than if these resources were installed throughout the school. It is also a safer solution if security is of great concern.

If resources are available for an ICT Coordinator, that staff member can assist the teacher with the technical aspects during class hours. Hardware, networks and software are prone to failure and these breakdowns are intimidating to a teacher asked to work in a technology lab. However, if help is on hand, the teacher can concentrate on the pedagogical aspects and leave the rest to the ICT Coordinator.

However, there are a number of drawbacks to this approach. The most important is that a technology lab, which is separated from the "normal" classroom, will be more intimidating to those teachers who are less comfortable working with technology or who feel uneasy with the expected increase of social interaction. These factors are magnified if no technical help is available in the room. A technology lab may be perceived as a major challenge by these teachers. The available machinery, in large numbers and with a prominent presence, may seem beyond his or her control. A technology lab does require some modification of an individual's teaching strategy, as well as a good knowledge of the software to be used. It also puts students more on their own, with generally more social interaction. A technology lab also makes it clear to a teacher that its software is their teaching partner.

Technology labs are also sometimes in great demand for use by many classes and this can make it difficult and frustrating for teachers to plan activities that require only short sessions with computers. A teacher should be able to work with a whole classroom at once without the burden of separating the class in two groups, leaving one group unattended, either in the classroom, or in the technology lab.

The technology lab plan might mix computers, portable keyboards and other devices (i.e. data loggers for science, digital microscopes, robotics devices and sensors, etc.) for student use, because for many tasks, students may need no more than a device with basic text processing capabilities or with some data storing functionality (i.e. for science projects).

Today, the availability of inexpensive wireless technology allows much more flexible deployment of educational resources inside a room. The Technology-in-the-classroom approach has a number of benefits, and it is one of the more favored solutions at present. The availability of the technology in the normal learning space has some important benefits because by its always being available, teachers can decide when to use it in more flexible ways, and can plan for its use in small, or large chunks of time, according to the educational needs and opportunities.

Fostering the teaching skills and attitudes to allow for a learning environment in which some students work with computers, keyboards or similar devices, perhaps in groups of two to four, others attend directly to the teacher and some others work on their own at their table, is a complex and time -consuming goal. This is not the typical frontal one-to-many classroom that many teachers are used to work with; rather it requires flexible approaches and a more interactive environment, where students are more actively cooperating to create more effective learning situations.

Many educational specialists favor constructivist methods to facilitate learning in these environments. Constructivist (and constructionist) methods seem to be particularly well-suited for mixed uses of diverse ICT devices. If not immediately used by teachers, they will at least help them in reflecting on their teaching methods and eventually to help move them towards more engaging learning environments.

Whatever decisions are made for the distribution of ICT inside a school in the early stages, a mixed decentralised approach should be seriously considered for the long run. ICT can play many roles effectively in a school, and in time, all professionals (teachers, administrators and librarians) will need and demand ICT for their work. Even if its advent is not consciously planned, ICT will be infused into schools over time, and, therefore it is most reasonable to plan for it in advance.

The distribution of equipment in many rooms throughout a school can pose security problems, such as hardware and software theft, tampering with files or misuse of information. If theft is a major concern, this approach can become very expensive in the long run. Also, if environmental conditions are poor inside the school (humidity, temperature, dust), then it might be preferable to proceed with a more centralised approach so these conditions can be controlled more effectively. These can be major drawbacks for this type of solution.

Maintaining equipment and software that is distributed all over the school might also increase costs and organisational effort, especially if teachers have little enthusiasm or skills to attend to and solve technical problems. The decentralised deployment of hardware will require additional training for all professionals involved. Supporting technical staff might also be required for maintenance and trouble-shooting tasks.

References

Dwyer, D., "Apple classroom of tomorrow: What we've learned", *Educational Leadership*, 1994.

Fullan, M. and A. Hargreaves, eds., *Teacher Development and Educational Change*, The Falmer Press, 1992.

Githiora-Updike, W., *The Global Schoolhouse*, in *The Digital Classroom*, D.T. Gordon, Editor. 2000,

Pelgrum, W.J., "Obstacles to the integration of ICT in education: results from a worldwide educational assessment" *Computers & Education*, 37: p. 163-178, 2001.

Venezky, R.L. and C. Davis, *Quo Vademus? The Transformation of Schooling in a Networked World*. 2002.

Zhao, Y., et al., *Conditions for Classroom Technology Innovation.* Teachers College Record, Columbia University, 2002.

Bibliography

Alfassi, A., Using information and communication technology (ICT) to foster literacy and facilitate discourse within the classroom, *Educational Media International*, vol. 37, no 3, 137-148, 2000.

Alspaugh, J. W., "The relationship between number of students per computer and educational outcomes", *Journal of Educational Computing Research*, *21*, 141-150, 1999.

Anderson, J., "The New Literacy and Technology", *Keynote address to the International Reading Association Convention*, San Antonio, Texas, April 1993.

Andrews, R., "Learning, literacy and ICT: what's the connection?" *English in Education*, vol. 34, no.3, 3-18, 2000.

Angus, L., Snyder, I. and Sutherland-Smith, W., "ICT and educational (dis)advantage: Families, computers and contemporary social and educational inequalities", *British Journal of Sociology of Education*, vol. 25, no 1, 3-18, 2004.

Barker, Roz, "The Internet and information skills—a primary school perspective", *Scan*, 15(1), February, pp.14-15, 1996.

Barkhouse, Nancy, "Grasping the thread: Web page development in the elementary classroom", *Emergency Librarian*, 24(3), January-February, pp.24-25, 1997.

Baron, L., D'Amico, M., Sissons, M., & Peters, P., "Attributions, group size and exposure time as predictors, of elementary children's performance on a microcomputer task", *Computers in Human Behavior*, *12*, 145-157, 1996.

Boling, Elizabeth and Kirkley, Sonny, "Helping students design World Wide Web documents", *TIE* (*Telecommunications in Education*) *News*, 8(4), August, pp.16-22, 1997.

Borton, W., "The effects of computer managed mastery learning on mathematics test scores in the elementary school", *Journal of Computer Based Instruction, 15*, 95-98, 1989.

Bracewell. R., Laferrière, T., Breuleux, A., Benoit, J., & Abdous, M., *The emerging contribution of online resources and tools to classroom learning and teaching*, Ottawa, Rescol Canada, 1998.

Burgstahler, Sheryl, *New Kids on the Net: A Network Sampler: Internet Activities for K-12*, Allyn and Bacon, New York, 1997.

Butterworth, Margaret, ed., *Information Technology in Schools: Implications for Teacher Librarians*, 3rd edn, Australian Library and Information Association, School Libraries Section (WA Group), Perth, 1997.

Carrucan, Tony, Tony, Crewe, Erica, Matthews, and Matthews, Matthews, *The Internet Manual for Teachers: Access Skills and Curriculum Strategies*, Macmillan Education, Melbourne, 1996.

Clarke, L. & Heaney, P., "Author online: Using asynchronous computer conferencing to support literacy", *British Journal of Educational Technology*, vol. 34, no. 1, 2003.

Clyde, Laurel A., "Yes, but what can we use it for? The Internet in school libraries", *Orana*, 33(2), May, pp.76-89, 1997

Coley, R., Cradler, J., & Engel, P., *Computers and Classrooms: The Status of Technology in US schools*, Princeton, NJ: Policy Information Center, Educational Testing Sevice, 1997.

D'Ignazio, Fred, "Think intranet", *Learning and Leading With Technology*, 24(1), September, pp.62-63, 1996.

Davies, Anne, *Making Classroom Assessment Work.* Merville, BC: Connections Publishing, 2000.

Drayton, B., & Falk, J. K., "Tell-tale signs of the inquiry-oriented classroom", *NASSP Bulletin,* 85(623), 24–34, 2001.

Dwyer, D., "Apple classroom of tomorrow: What we've learned", *Educational Leadership*, 1994.

Eade, Jan, "Internet for novices", *Scan*, 15(2), May, pp.56-62, 1996.

Eisner, Elliot W., "The Uses and Limits of Performance Assessment", *Phi Delta Kappan* 80, 9, pp. 658–660, 1999.

Farnham-Diggory, S., *Schooling*, Harvard University Press, Cambridge, MA., 1990.

Friedhoff, R. and Benzon, W., "Visualisation: The Second Computer Revolution", Harry N. Abrams, New York, 1989.

Fullan, M. and A. Hargreaves, eds., *Teacher Development and Educational Change*, The Falmer Press, 1992.

Gardner, H., *Frames of Mind: The Theory of Multiple Intelligences*, Basic Books, New York, 1983.

_______________ , *The Unschooled Mind: How children think and how schools should teach*, Basic Books, New York, 1991.

_______________ , *Multiple Intelligences: The Theory in Practice*, New York, NY: BasicBooks, 1993.

Githiora-Updike, W., *The Global Schoolhouse*, in *The Digital Classroom*, D.T. Gordon, Editor. 2000,

Glasscock, Alison, "The Internet and information skills—a secondary perspective", *Scan*, 15(1), February, pp.16-17, 1996.

Gregory, Kathleen, Caren Cameron and Anne Davies, *Knowing What Counts, Book Two—Self- Assessment and Goal Setting: For Use in Middle and Secondary School Classrooms*, Merville, BC: Connections Publishing, 2000.

Guskey, Thomas R. "Reporting on Student Learning: Lessons from the Past—Prescriptions for the Future". In Thomas R. Guskey (ed.), *Communicating Student Learning: 1996 ASCD Yearbook*, pp. 13–24, 1996

Hacker, D.J., "Metacognition: Definitions and empirical foundations", *The MIT encyclopedia of cognitive sciences,* 1999.

Heineke, W.F. and Blasi, L. (Eds)., *Methods of Evaluating Educational Technology*, Information Age Publishing, Greenwich, Connecticut, 2001.

Johnson, Doug, "Student access to Internet: librarians and teachers working together to teach higher level survival skills", *Emergency Librarian,* 22(3), January-February, pp.8-12, 1995.

Jonassen, David H., Kyle L. Peck and Brent G. Wilson, *Learning With Technology: a constructivist perspective*, Upper Saddle River, NJ: Prentice Hall, 1999.

Koivusaari, R., "Cognitive strategies and computer-supported learning environments", *Educational Psychology*, vol. 19, no. 3, 309-116, 1999.

Krishnamurthy R.C., *Network-based Teaching and Learning*, Authorspress, New Delhi, 2004.

Kuhlthau, C. C., & D. Oberg (Eds.), *Inquiry-based learning: Lessons from Library Power* (pp. 13–30).

Lanham, R.A., "What's next for text?" *Education, Communication and Information*. vol. 1, no. 1, 2001.

Lankshear, C. and Knobel, M., "New technologies in early childhood literacy research: A review of research", *Journal of Early Childhood Literacy*, vol. 3, 59-82, 2003.

McCullen, Caroline, "World Wide Web in the classroom: the quintessential collaboration", *Learning and Leading With Technology*, 23(3), November, pp.7-10, 1995.

Mumford, L., *The Myth of The Machine: Technics and Human Development*, Harcourt, Brace and World, New York, 1967.

Ormes, S., The use and importance of the internet in literature-based services in children's libraries, *Electronic Library*, vol. 16, no 6, 379-385, 1998.

Papert, S., *Mindstorms: Children, Computers, and Powerful Ideas*, Basic Books, New York, 1981.

Passey, D. and Rogers, C., *The motivational effects of ICT on pupils*, London: DfES, 2004.

Pelgrum, W.J., "Obstacles to the integration of ICT in education: results from a worldwide educational assessment" *Computers & Education*, 37: p. 163-178, 2001.

Perelman, L.J., *School's Out: Hyperlearning, The New Technology, and the End of Education*, William Morrow and Company, New York, 1992.

Plowman, L. and Stephen, C., A 'benign addition'? Research on ICT and pre-school children, *Journal of Computer Assisted Learning*, 19, no 2, 149-164, 2003.

Popham, W. James, *The Truth About Testing: An Educator's Call to Action*, Alexandria, VA: Association for Supervision and Curriculum Development, 2001.

Ross, Tweed W. and Bailey, Gerald D., "Creating safe Internet access", *Learning and Leading With Technology*, 24(1), September, pp.51-53, 1996.

Scrimshaw, P., "Computers and literacy: effeciency, extension or transformation?" *Literacy Today*, no. 25, 10, 2000.

Selwyn, N. and Bullon, K., "Primary school children's use of ICT", *British Journal of Educational Technology*, vol. 31, no. 4., 2000.

Sternberg, R.J., *The Triarchic Mind: A New Theory of Intelligence*, Viking Press, New York, 1988.

Stiggins, Richard J., *Student-Involved Classroom Assessment (Third Edition)*, Upper Saddle River, NJ: Prentice-Hall, Inc., 2001.

Stix, Andi, *Strategies for Student-Centered Assessment*, New Rochelle, NY: The Interactive Classroom, 1996.

Talesra, Hemlata, Shukul and Sharma, *Challenges of Education: Technology, Trends, Globalisation*, Authorspress, 2003.

UNESCO, *Information and Communication Technologies in Schools, A Handbook for Teachers*, 2005.

________________, *Information and Communication Technologies in Teacher Education: A Planning Guide* (Ed. P. Resta), UNESCO, Paris, 2002.

________________, *Information and Communication Technology in Education: A Curriculum for Schools and Programme of Teacher Development* (Eds. J. Anderson and T. van Weert), 2002.

Venezky, R.L. and C. Davis, *Quo Vademus? The Transformation of Schooling in a Networked World*. 2002.

Watts, M., and Lloyd, C., The use of innovative ICT in the active pursuit of literacy, *Journal of Computer Assisted Learning*, vol. 20, no 1, 50-58, 2004.

Wiggins, Grant and Jay McTighe, *Understanding by Design*, Alexandria, VA: Association for Supervision and Curriculum Development, 1998.

Worthington, OH: Linworth, Jonassen, David H., *Computers as mindtools for schools: Engaging critical thinking* (2nd ed.), 2000.

Zhao, Y., et al., *Conditions for Classroom Technology Innovation*. Teachers College Record, Columbia University, 2002.

Index